PUBLISHERS' NOTE

As its title implies, the Series in which this volume appears has two purposes. One is to encourage the publication of monographs on advanced or specialised topics in, or related to, the theory and applications of probability and statistics; such works may sometimes be more suited to the present form of publication because the topic may not have reached the stage where a comprehensive treatment is desirable. The second purpose is to make available to a wider public concise courses in the field of probability and statistics, which are sometimes based on unpublished lectures.

The Series was edited from its inception in 1957 by Professor Maurice G. Kendall, under whose editorship the first 21 volumes in the Series appeared. He was succeeded as editor in 1965 by Professor Alan Stuart.

The publishers will be interested in approaches from any authors who have work of importance suitable for the Series.

CHARLES GRIFFIN & CO. LTD.

GRIFFIN'S STATISTICAL MONOGRAPHS AND COURSES

No. 5, formerly *Characteristic Functions* by E. Lukacs, is now published independently of the Series

For a list of other statistical and mathematical books see back cover.

ECONOMETRIC TECHNIQUES AND PROBLEMS

C. E. V. LESER

Dr. Phil., M.Sc. (Econ.)

Professor of Econometrics, University of Leeds

BEING NUMBER TWENTY OF
GRIFFIN'S STATISTICAL
MONOGRAPHS & COURSES

EDITED BY

ALAN STUART, D.Sc. (Econ.)

Second edition

GRIFFIN 18 20 LONDON

CHARLES GRIFFIN & COMPANY LIMITED
42 DRURY LANE, LONDON, WC2B 5RX

First published   1966
Second impression (with minor corrections)   1969
Third impression   1972
Second edition   1974

Demy Octavo, viii+144 pages
ISBN 0 85264 218 0

Printed in Great Britain by
Whitstable Litho, Straker Brothers Ltd

PREFACE TO FIRST EDITION

This book is based on a course of lectures which were held, together with exercises and discussion, at the Economic Research Institute, Dublin, in the winter of 1963–64. Participants in the course were mainly university students of economics in their honours year and economics graduates in the public service, in business, and in research institutes. It is hoped that a modified written version will be of interest to a wider public of economics students and ex-students having some, but not necessarily an extensive, knowledge of mathematics and statistics, and who wish to get a good grasp of what econometrics is and how it is used. At the same time, it is hoped that the book will provide an introduction for students who intend to specialize in econometrics and allied subjects later on, and who will follow it up by more detailed study.

I am greatly indebted to Dr R. C. Geary, Director of the Economic Research Institute, Dublin, to Professor Lester D. Taylor, of Harvard University, and to Professor J. Waelbroeck, of the Université Libre de Bruxelles, for reading the draft version and for making many valuable comments and suggestions for improvement. I am also much indebted to Miss Anna MacMahon for typing the script and for helping with the proof-reading.

C. E. V. LESER

THE ECONOMIC RESEARCH INSTITUTE, DUBLIN
February, 1966

PREFACE TO SECOND EDITION

Shortly after the appearance in print of this book, I returned to university teaching and found that I could use the book as a basis for a third-year course given to economics students who had pursued mathematics to A-level or its equivalent and who had followed statistics courses for two years. Some shortcomings of the first edition also became apparent, and the present version represents an attempt to remedy them.

Among other things, new sections on modifications of least-squares regression, on dummy variables and parallel regressions, and on model-building problems have been introduced into Chapters 2, 3 and 7 respectively. Section 4.4 has been expanded to include an account of the limited-information maximum-likelihood method. Chapter 5 on production functions has been virtually rewritten, introducing much additional material. In Chapter 6, the section on analysis of market data has been expanded to include demand and supply models. Some of the recent work in various fields has been reviewed.

There is now a much wider choice of econometrics textbooks available to the reader than at the time when the first edition was written. It is hoped that this book, which aims at presenting essentials of method and applications whilst avoiding frightening length, can still make its contribution to learning and comprehension in this field.

UNIVERSITY OF LEEDS   C. E. V. LESER
August, 1973

CONTENTS

Introduction

1. MEANING AND SCOPE

Econometrics is a comparatively young branch of science, known by this name only since the 1930's. The year 1930 saw the foundation of the Econometric Society, which describes itself as " an international society for the advancement of economic theory in its relation to statistics and mathematics ". Since 1933 the society has published its journal *Econometrica* which has served as an important though by no means the only medium for the publication of econometric studies. There have been earlier studies which we would nowadays describe as econometric, notably the pioneer works of Moore (1914, 1917). Nevertheless it is true to say that a substantial body of econometric research has only been carried out since the 1940s and that many of the results, particularly in the applied field, cannot yet be considered as well established.

Literally, of course, econometrics means economic measurement, and measurement is an important element of econometrics; but not all economic measurement is regarded as econometrics. The estimation of national income or the construction of a retail price index are important problems of measurement but not econometric problems. At one time, more or less all economic applications of mathematical methods were regarded as econometrics by some authors, for example in the textbook by Davis (1941); but nowadays a more restricted view of the subject-matter is generally accepted.

Econometrics may, perhaps, be defined as the discipline which attempts the establishment of quantitative relationships between economic variables with the aid of statistical methods. The wording may be varied and indeed varies in the textbooks which give a definition. What is important is to get an idea about the subject-matter and the features which distinguish it from adjoining disciplines.

The words " quantitative " (or " numerical "), " relationships ", and " economic " may be regarded as the keywords as they provide the demarcation lines from mathematical economics, descriptive economic statistics, and statistical theory. Mathematical economics, which is really economic theory formulated mathematically, studies the relationships between economic variables but in algebraic terms or with assumed numerical values of constants; it becomes econometrics when these numerical values are estimated from observation.

1

Descriptive economic statistics applies quantitative measurement to economic variables, but does not attempt to establish relationships between them. Statistical theory and method is concerned with the study of relationships between variables, but unless applied to economic theory or economic analysis it does not become econometrics.

There are two kinds of econometrics: econometric methods on the one hand, and their application to specific economic problems on the other. The methods used in econometrics are basically those of regression analysis, which forms part of ordinary statistical theory and method, though the nature of the problems encountered here brings a particular slant to the approach adopted, as well as extensions of conventional statistics which were specially developed for the present purpose. The relationships which are investigated with the aid of these methods, like demand functions and production functions, lie at the very heart of economic theory, though the particular form of relationship chosen in a particular study may well constitute an innovation. Thus it would be legitimate to treat econometrics either as a branch of statistics or as a branch of economics.

This duality creates some problems for the teaching of econometrics. If econometric methods are mainly studied, there is the danger of losing sight of the fields in which the methods are applied; if economic applications are immediately tackled, a full treatment will require long methodological digressions. The majority of textbooks emphasize the methodological aspect, supplementing it to a greater or lesser extent by economic illustrations. Books in this category which have stood the test of time include those by Christ (1967) and Johnston (1972), and on a more advanced level, those by Goldberger (1964) and Malinvaud (1970). As against this, the approach to econometrics through the medium of economic applications is followed by Klein (1962), Cramer (1969) and Bridge (1971).

In the present volume, the approach is, in the first part, to review or introduce the statistical techniques used, and to follow on with a study of selected problems of applied econometrics in the second part. The introductory text by Walters (1970) follows the same plan as this book. Whilst comprehensiveness cannot be claimed for a book of this size, it is hoped it will provide an introduction to either kind of problem facing the econometrician. For further reading, students are referred to the books mentioned in the preceding paragraph; see also Leser (1971a).

Mathematics enters econometrics at two stages: in the formulation of theoretical relationships, and in the development or justification of statistical techniques. Econometrics cannot be regarded as a branch of mathematics, but mathematics plays an important part in it. It is the

2

synthesis of mathematics, economics and statistics that makes econometrics into the powerful, or at any rate potentially powerful, tool that it is. With the aid of econometrics, economic theories may be disproved as unrealistic, or at least shown to be inapplicable in a particular setting. Whilst econometrics cannot prove a theory, it can show it to be consistent with observation; and it can give it greater depth by providing numerical values for parameters in the equations, the more so as in some instances these values profoundly influence the character of the relationship. Econometric equations may be important for forecasting, or for assessing the effect of policy decisions at the level of firm or government, such as a price change or a modification of a tax rate.

The mathematical treatment of econometrics may be at different levels, according to the extent to which refined methods are introduced and rigorous proofs are desired. Much of the existing literature is fairly mathematical and abstract, and for its reading a good mathematical equipment is required, in particular a thorough knowledge of matrix algebra. If mathematics is a kind of shorthand, the notation of matrix algebra may be considered as a super-shorthand; whilst the latter is useful, it is not considered as essential for the purpose of the present volume, as presentation in greater detail should aid understanding. The main knowledge of mathematics assumed, apart from general familiarity with algebraic symbols and functions, will be a knowledge of the differential calculus, and of determinants with their elementary properties.

Similarly, some familiarity with the most important statistical concepts, such as random variables, standard errors, and significance, and particularly those of regression analysis, will be assumed; a knowledge of estimation theory will be a help. A good acquaintance with the concepts of economics is also important. Econometrics is not a first-year university subject; generally students are expected to have acquired some knowledge of mathematics, statistics and economics before they tackle it. Nevertheless, it is not necessary to become an expert in all these subjects in order to acquire an appreciation of the problems with which econometrics and the user of econometric methods are confronted.

In the first part of the book, simple regression, multiple regression, and simultaneous equation estimation are successively discussed. Emphasis will be on reasoning and the underlying assumptions of the methods, rather than on mathematical rigour. The methods are illustrated by numerical examples which are based on actual data and which represent highly simplified versions of actual or possible econometric studies.

3

In the second part, three sets of econometric problems are considered successively; they are (a) the construction of production functions, (b) demand analysis, and (c) model building for an economy as a whole. This list does not exhaust all possible topics, but more of them may be considered under these headings if they are suitably extended. In this part of the book, emphasis is laid on the results obtained and their limitations.

It is believed that the methods and results given will become more real to the reader if he carries out some computation and interpretation himself at suitable points. The reader is therefore invited to attempt the exercises which are interspersed in the text before proceeding any further in the perusal. Answers or suggested answers are given at the end of each chapter but should preferably be used as a check only.

Input–output analysis is counted as mathematical economics rather than econometrics and is therefore not covered here, though its possible use in connection with econometric studies may be noted. Studies of the distribution of income, which are treated as econometric problems by some authors, are also considered here as falling outside the main field, though having a bearing on econometrics. There is not invariably a clear-cut border line between econometrics and neighbouring disciplines, but the three topics of production functions, demand functions, and macro-economic models are certainly central ones to the discipline under consideration here.

The survey of approaches to econometric problems may tend to show that many of the findings are highly tentative. This state of affairs lies in the nature of the problems and of the statistical material used in the attempted solutions, and it means that a good deal of further work is required. Whilst showing the difficulties which econometrics has to face, the discussion of econometric problems will, it is hoped, also underline the potentialities of the econometric approach.

PART I: METHODS

2. SIMPLE REGRESSION

2.1 Estimation of regression coefficients

Given two variables x' and y', it is assumed that between them there exists a theoretical linear relationship of the form

$$y' = \alpha + \beta x'$$

where α and β are constants. x' and y' may directly represent economic variables like price and demand, or those variables after a logarithmic or other transformation. Thus a wide range of functional relationships between the original economic variables is covered by this approach.

Furthermore, let n pairs of observations (x'_1, y'_1), (x'_2, y'_2), ... , (x'_n, y'_n) be given. They may refer to different periods of time, different areas, different industries, etc. Owing to what we may call errors or disturbances, the relationship between the observations is not exact but of the form

$$y'_i = \alpha + \beta x'_i + \varepsilon_i \qquad (i = 1, 2, \dots n) \qquad (2.1)$$

where ε_i is an independently distributed random variable with mean 0 and variance σ^2.

The problem is to estimate the values of the constants α and β. The classical approach is to use the method of least squares; if the observations are plotted on a scatter diagram, the line representing the equation is so chosen that the sum of squares of the vertical distances between the points and the line is a minimum.

Here and in future, x_i and y_i denote the deviations of the observations from their arithmetic means, and all summations unless otherwise indicated are taken over all observations. Thus

$$\bar{x}' = \Sigma x'/n \qquad \bar{y}' = \Sigma y'/n$$

$$x_i = x'_i - \bar{x}' \qquad y_i = y'_i - \bar{y}'$$

The relationship (2.1) then becomes

$$y_i = \beta x_i + \varepsilon_i - \bar{\varepsilon} \qquad (2.2)$$

The least-squares estimates for α and β are written as a and b. Then

$$b = \Sigma xy / \Sigma x^2 \qquad (2.3)$$

$$a = \bar{y}' - b\bar{x}' = (\Sigma y' - b\Sigma x')/n \qquad (2.4)$$

5

For practical computation, use is made of the short-cut formulae

$$\left.\begin{array}{l} \Sigma\,x^2 = \Sigma\,x'^2 - (\Sigma\,x')^2/n \\[4pt] \Sigma\,xy = \Sigma\,x'y' - \Sigma\,x'\,\Sigma\,y'/n \end{array}\right\} \tag{2.5}$$

which obviate the need to compute individual deviations from means. Sometimes the computation of $n\Sigma\,x^2$ and $n\Sigma\,xy$ is preferred; their ratio, of course, also yields b.

This is all familiar ground even for students of elementary statistical methods only, and is described in most statistical textbooks or in special treatises on regression, such as those by Ezekiel and Fox (1959) and by Williams (1959). The reasons why this method is chosen in preference to any other are less familiar, nor is it generally realized what implicit assumptions had to be made for its legitimate use.

An alternative estimate b' which is much easier to compute than b is obtained by assuming all x_i' to be arranged in ascending order and writing

$$b' = (y_n' - y_1')/(x_n' - x_1') \tag{2.6}$$

Geometrically, this means connecting the two points farthest to the left and farthest to the right on the scatter diagram by a straight line.

It is easily seen that b' yields an unbiased estimate of β, since we can write, from (2.1) and (2.6),

$$b' = [\beta(x_n' - x_1') + (\varepsilon_n - \varepsilon_1)]/(x_n' - x_1')$$
$$= \beta + (\varepsilon_n - \varepsilon_1)/(x_n' - x_1')$$

and since $E(\varepsilon_1) = E(\varepsilon_n) = 0$ we have for its expectation $E(b')$

$$E(b') = \beta$$

The main drawback of b' is that its estimate of β does not automatically and indefinitely gain in accuracy if further observations are added; in statistical terminology, b' is not a consistent estimator of β. This can be seen from its sampling variance

$$V(b') = E\{(b' - \beta)\}^2$$
$$= E(\varepsilon_n - \varepsilon_1)^2/(x_n' - x_1')^2$$

Thus by a well-known statistical theorem

$$V(b') = 2\sigma^2/(x_n' - x_1')^2 \tag{2.7}$$

which need not tend towards 0 with increasing n as the variable x may be bounded. The point seems intuitively clear from the fact that most of the information given by the data is ignored in making the estimate.

6

In contrast to b', the least-square estimator b is unbiased and consistent; we have from (2.2) and (2.3)

$$b = (\beta \, \Sigma \, x^2 + \Sigma \, \varepsilon x)/\Sigma \, x^2$$
$$= \beta + \Sigma \, \varepsilon x/\Sigma \, x^2$$
$$E(b) = \beta$$
$$V(b) = E\{(\Sigma \, \varepsilon x)^2\}/(\Sigma \, x^2)^2$$

and since only the expectations of the squares of ε, not its cross-products, are different from 0 and equal to σ^2,

$$V(b) = \sigma^2 \, \Sigma \, x^2/(\Sigma \, x^2)^2$$
$$= \sigma^2/\Sigma \, x^2 \tag{2.8}$$

which tends to 0 with increasing n as $\Sigma \, x^2$ takes in more and more terms.

There are other estimators which are unbiased and consistent. One which is sometimes used in practical work is that yielded by the three-group method, which was developed by Wald (1940) and Bartlett (1949), though originally with a view to avoiding bias in connection with errors in x. For this purpose, the observations are again arranged in order of x_i' and divided into three equal parts (or approximately equal ones if n is not divisible by 3). Then the arithmetic means $\bar{x}_1'$, $\bar{y}_1'$ for the lowest group and $\bar{x}_3'$, $\bar{y}_3'$ for the highest group are computed, i.e.

$$\bar{x}_1' = 3 \sum_{1}^{n/3} x'/n \qquad \bar{y}_1' = 3 \sum_{1}^{n/3} y'/n$$

$$\bar{x}_3' = 3 \sum_{2n/3+1}^{n} x'/n \qquad \bar{y}_3' = 3 \sum_{2n/3+1}^{n} y'/n$$

and the three-group estimator b'' is given as

$$b'' = (\bar{y}_3' - \bar{y}_1')/(\bar{x}_3' - \bar{x}_1')$$
$$= \left(\sum_{2n/3+1}^{n} y' - \sum_{1}^{n/3} y' \right) \Big/ \left(\sum_{2n/3+1}^{n} x' - \sum_{1}^{n/3} x' \right) \tag{2.9}$$

From (2.1), with $\bar{\varepsilon}_1$ and $\bar{\varepsilon}_3$ defined in analogy with $\bar{x}_1'$, $\bar{y}_1'$, $\bar{x}_3'$, $\bar{y}_3'$,

$$b'' = \beta + (\bar{\varepsilon}_3 - \bar{\varepsilon}_1)/(\bar{x}_3' - \bar{x}_1')$$
$$E(b'') = \beta$$

Since $\bar{\varepsilon}_1$ and $\bar{\varepsilon}_3$ are means of $n/3$ terms,

$$E(\bar{\varepsilon}_1^2) = E(\bar{\varepsilon}_3^2) = 3\sigma^2/n$$

$$V(b'') = 6\sigma^2/n(\bar{x}_3' - \bar{x}_1')^2 \tag{2.10}$$

which tends to 0 with increasing n.

It may well be asked why the three-group method is preferred to a two-group method in which one divides the data into two equal groups and from then on proceeds as before, thus utilizing all data in the estimator. The answer is that with equally spaced data, the three-group method is the more efficient, that is to say, it gives a smaller sampling variance than the two-group method; in other cases the relative efficiency depends on the distribution. In fact, in this case of equally spaced data the method is nearly as efficient as least squares.

Exercise 2.1 Show that with equally spaced data (say $x'_1 = 1, \dots, x'_n = n$), $V(b'')$ is only about one-eighth greater than $V(b)$.

The computational burden is somewhat less with b'' than with b. Nevertheless, in scientific work where these considerations are not of overriding importance, least-squares methods are generally used. The reason is that under the usual assumptions, b is the best unbiased linear estimator of β', i.e. the estimator with the smallest sampling variance. This is a special case of what is known as the Gauss–Markoff theorem; the proof in this case is simple.

Write b' for the estimator which must be in the general form

$$b' = \Sigma \, w'y'$$
$$= (\alpha \Sigma \, w' + \beta \Sigma \, w'x' + \Sigma \, w'\varepsilon)$$

Necessary and sufficient for $E(b') = \beta$ are the conditions

$$\Sigma \, w' = 0$$
$$\Sigma \, w'x' = 1 \quad \text{for all values of } x'$$

This is easily seen to be possible only if we can write $w' = w/\Sigma \, wx'$. Then

$$b' = \beta + \Sigma \, w\varepsilon/\Sigma \, wx'$$
$$V(b') = \sigma^2 \Sigma \, w^2/(\Sigma \, wx)^2$$

This is a minimum, subject to $\Sigma \, w = 0$, if for all i

$$\frac{\partial}{\partial w_i} \{\sigma^2 \, \Sigma \, w^2/(\Sigma \, wx)^2 - \lambda \Sigma \, w\} = 0$$
$$2w_i/\Sigma \, w^2 - 2x'_i/\Sigma \, wx' = \lambda'$$

where

$$\lambda' = \lambda(\Sigma \, wx)^2/\sigma^2 \, \Sigma \, w^2$$

or

$$w_i = cx'_i + c'$$

λ, λ', c and c' being the same for all i. Furthermore, to satisfy the condition $\Sigma \, w = 0$,

$$w_i = c(x'_i - \bar{x}'_i) = cx_i$$
$$b' = \Sigma \, xy'/\Sigma \, xx'$$
$$= \Sigma \, xy/\Sigma \, x^2$$
$$= b$$

8

i.e. the least-square estimator is best. Similarly, a is the best unbiased linear estimator of α.

In connection with least-square computation of b and a, a few further calculations are usually made. The coefficient of determination r^2, showing the proportion of the variance of y which is explained by the regression, and which also represents the square of the ordinary correlation coefficient r, is obtained by the formula

$$r^2 = b \Sigma xy / \Sigma y^2 \qquad (2.11)$$

where

$$\Sigma y^2 = \Sigma y'^2 - (\Sigma y')^2 / n$$

This measures the goodness of fit and provides one criterion for deciding whether to be content with the result or to search further for a better solution.

Also, if u_i is the residual after regression,

$$u_i = y_i' - a - bx_i' = y_i - bx_i$$

we find that

$$\Sigma u^2 = \Sigma y^2 - b \Sigma xy \qquad (2.12)$$

and the ratio

$$s^2 = \Sigma u^2 / (n-2) \qquad (2.13)$$

provides an estimate of the theoretical error variance. Thus the standard error of b can be estimated as

$$s_b = \sqrt{s^2 / \Sigma x^2} \qquad (2.14)$$

This is used, together with Student's t-distribution for $n-2$ degrees of freedom, to construct confidence limits or to test the significance of b. For tabulations of this or a related distribution, one may refer to a textbook of statistics, or to Lindley and Miller (1953) or Murdoch and Barnes (1968).

It may also be shown that

$$s_a = \sqrt{s^2/(1/n + \bar{x}^2 / \Sigma x^2)} = \sqrt{s^2 \Sigma x'^2 / n \Sigma x^2} \qquad (2.15)$$

For the application of the t-distribution it is necessary to assume that the errors are normally distributed, or at any rate approximately so. The optimal property of unbiasedness and minimum variance which b and also a possess does not depend on the assumption of normality.

There is another sense in which the least-squares estimators can be said to represent an optimum, though for this it is again necessary to assume normality of the error distribution. Under this assumption a and b can be shown to be maximum-likelihood estimators for α and β. This means that if α and β have the values a and b, the probability density for obtaining the values (x_1', y_1'), ..., (x_n', y_n') which were actually

9

observed, is greater than with any other values assumed by α and β. Maximum-likelihood estimators, in general, although not necessarily unbiased, are consistent and fully efficient and thus in a sense optimal.

With normally distributed errors, the likelihood function is

$$L = (2\pi)^{-n/2}\sigma^{-n} \exp\{-\Sigma(y'-\alpha-\beta x')^2/2\sigma^2\}$$
$$-\log L = n \log(2\pi)/2 + n \log \sigma + \Sigma(y'-\alpha-\beta x')^2/2\sigma^2$$

L is maximized when $-\log L$ is minimized. But this is achieved when the sum of squares $\Sigma(y'-\alpha-\beta x')^2$ is minimized, or in other words by least squares. Incidentally, the maximum-likelihood estimate of σ^2 is $\Sigma u^2/n$ which is biased, the unbiased estimate being $s^2 = \Sigma u^2/(n-2)$. Before going any farther and considering cases in which the argument followed here is not valid, the formulae given may be illustrated by means of a numerical example.

Example 2.1 According to the C.S.O. (1971), figures for personal income x' and personal savings y' in the United Kingdom, rounded and in £000 mill., are as follows:

Year	x'	y'
1949	10·5	·12
1950	11·0	·13
1951	11·9	·11
1952	12·7	·38
1953	13·5	·42
1954	14·3	·37
1955	15·5	·47
1956	16·6	·76
1957	17·5	·75
1958	18·5	·62
1959	19·6	·82
1960	21·2	1·22
1961	22·9	1·70
1962	24·1	1·57
1963	25·6	1·62
1964	27·7	1·77
1965	30·1	1·97
1966	32·1	2·13
1967	33·7	2·12
1968	36·3	2·06
1969	38·8	2·40
1970	42·8	2·79

10

A linear regression of savings on income is assumed. By the alternative methods described, various estimates for the regression coefficients can be obtained.

As it happens, the observations are arranged in ascending order of x', so that we immediately get

$$b' = (2 \cdot 79 - \cdot 12)/(42 \cdot 8 - 10 \cdot 5) = 2 \cdot 67/32 \cdot 3$$

$$= \cdot 082\,66$$

Furthermore, with 22 observations

$$\sum_{1}^{7} x' = 89 \cdot 4 \qquad \sum_{1}^{7} y' = 2 \cdot 00$$

$$\sum_{16}^{22} x' = 241 \cdot 5 \qquad \sum_{16}^{22} y' = 15 \cdot 24$$

$$b'' = (15 \cdot 24 - 2 \cdot 00)/(241 \cdot 5 - 89 \cdot 4) = 13 \cdot 24/152 \cdot 5$$

$$= \cdot 086\,82$$

The least-squares computations yield

$$\Sigma x' = 496 \cdot 9$$
$$\Sigma y' = 26 \cdot 30$$
$$\Sigma x'^2 = 13\,173 \cdot 75$$
$$\Sigma x'y' = 759 \cdot 910$$
$$\Sigma y'^2 = 46 \cdot 2194$$

Thus $\quad \Sigma x^2 = 13\,173 \cdot 75 - (496 \cdot 9)^2/22 = 13\,173 \cdot 75 - 11\,223 \cdot 16$
$$= 1950 \cdot 6$$
$$\Sigma xy = 759 \cdot 910 - 496 \cdot 9 \times 26 \cdot 30/22 = 759 \cdot 910 - 594 \cdot 021$$
$$= 165 \cdot 89$$
$$\Sigma y^2 = 46 \cdot 2194 - 26 \cdot 30^2/22 = 46 \cdot 2194 - 31 \cdot 4405$$
$$= 14 \cdot 779$$
$$b = 165 \cdot 89/1950 \cdot 6$$
$$= \cdot 08505$$

The three estimates of β are fairly close together, but b' is further apart from b'' and b than are b'' and b to each other. The strong dependence of b' on extreme values may also be shown in a different way.

11

Exercise 2.2 Verify that a 10% adjustment to the 1970 savings figure would alter the value of b' by more than 10% but that of b'' and b only by 2–3½%.

Although b'' gives a good estimate of β, nevertheless here and in future the least-squares method will be used for the reasons outlined, and also because it lends itself admirably to further computations and extensions. At this stage a cross-check on the calculations is opportune. In this example, we could write down a column of figures for the combination $x' + 10\,y'$, derive the value of

$$\Sigma(x+10y)^2 = \Sigma(x'+10y')^2 - [\Sigma(x'+10y')]^2/n$$
$$= 32993\cdot89 - 26247\cdot63 = 6746\cdot3$$

and verify that by adding Σx^2, $20\Sigma xy$ and $100\Sigma y^2$, we reach the same total. With $b = \cdot08505$ we obtain from (2.4)

$$a = (26\cdot30 - \cdot08505 \times 496\cdot9)/22 = -15\cdot9613/22$$
$$= -\cdot7255$$

so that the theoretical relationship between income Y and savings S is estimated as

$$S_c = -\cdot7255 + \cdot08505\,Y$$

Also $\qquad b\Sigma xy = 14\cdot109$

and from (2.12), (2.13) and (2.14)

$$\Sigma u^2 = 14\cdot779 - 14\cdot109$$
$$= \cdot670$$
$$s^2 = \cdot670/20$$
$$= \cdot0335$$
$$s_b = \sqrt{\cdot0335/1950\cdot6} = \sqrt{\cdot00001717}$$
$$= \cdot00414$$

b is therefore significantly different from zero at any reasonable level, and 95 per cent confidence limits for β are

$$\cdot08505 - 2\cdot09 \times \cdot00414 \leqslant \beta \leqslant \cdot08505 + 2\cdot09 \times \cdot00414$$
$$\cdot0764 \leqslant \beta \leqslant \cdot0937$$

Also, from (2.15)

$$s_a = \sqrt{\cdot0335 \times 13173\cdot75/22 \times 1950\cdot6}$$
$$= \sqrt{441\cdot32/42913} = \sqrt{\cdot010284}$$
$$= \cdot1014$$

12

Therefore a is also highly significant.

Note that all these conclusions are only valid if the specification of a linear relationship between income and savings is really correct as it stands. This cannot be taken for granted; on the contrary, there are good reasons for doubting it.

From (2.11) we also derive the result

$$r^2 = 14 \cdot 109/14 \cdot 779$$
$$= \cdot 955$$

This seems to indicate a good fit. To a large extent, however, it only shows the long-term increase over time common to both series, due to both price rises and economic growth in real terms. This should be borne in mind when interpreting the result.

Exercise 2.3 Replace the income series in Example 2.1 by time in years ($x' = 1, 2, ..., 22$). Show that a regression on time explains the variations in personal savings as well as a regression on personal income.

2.2 Modifications of least-squares regression

Sometimes the linear relationship between the variables x' and y' is known or can be assumed to have no constant term, so that the regression line passes through the origin on the scatter diagram. Writing

$$y'_i = \beta x'_i + \varepsilon_i$$

the least-squares estimator of β then is

$$b = \Sigma x'y'/\Sigma x'^2 \qquad (2.16)$$

Clearly $\qquad\qquad E(b) = \beta$

and $\qquad\qquad V(b) = \sigma^2/\Sigma x'^2$

Since $\Sigma x'^2 > \Sigma x^2$ (except when $\Sigma x' = 0$), the sampling variance of b is smaller than that obtained from the same data without this restriction being imposed upon the regression. This is not surprising. Furthermore

$$u_i = y'_i - bx'_i$$
$$\Sigma u^2 = \Sigma y'^2 - b\Sigma x'y' \qquad (2.17)$$

and since the regression now absorbs only one degree of freedom

$$s^2 = \Sigma u^2/(n-1) \qquad (2.18)$$
$$s_b = \sqrt{s^2/\Sigma x'^2} \qquad (2.19)$$

13

which is used together with Student's distribution for $n-1$ degrees of freedom.

In Example 2.1, the constant term a is significant, and a regression without constant term would not be appropriate when constructed from the original data. The relationship may, however, be formulated in a somewhat different way, to the effect that the year-to-year changes ΔY in personal income and ΔS in personal savings are related to each other. It then seems reasonable to put ΔS as proportionate to ΔY apart from a disturbance term. Denoting now ΔY by x' and ΔS by y', the variables are

x'	y'	x'	y'
·5	·01	1·7	·48
·9	−·02	1·2	−·13
·8	·27	1·5	·05
·8	·04	2·1	·15
·8	−·05	2·4	·20
1·2	·10	2·0	·16
1·1	·29	1·6	−·01
·9	−·01	2·6	−·06
1·0	−·13	2·5	·34
1·1	·20	4·0	·39
1·6	·40		

There is one observation fewer than with the original variables, but the same degrees of freedom are available for the estimation of σ^2 ($n = 21$, $n-1 = 20$). Calculation yields the results

$$\Sigma x'^2 = 63\!\cdot\!53$$
$$\Sigma x'y' = 5\!\cdot\!443$$
$$\Sigma y'^2 = \cdot9979$$

and from (2.16), (2.17), (2.18) and (2.19)

$$b = 5\!\cdot\!443/63\!\cdot\!53$$
$$= \cdot08568$$
$$\Sigma u^2 = \cdot9979 - \cdot08568 \times 5\!\cdot\!443$$
$$= \cdot5315$$
$$s^2 = \cdot5315/20$$
$$= \cdot026575$$
$$s_b = \sqrt{\cdot026575/63\!\cdot\!53} = \sqrt{\cdot00041831}$$
$$= \cdot0205$$

Hence: $\quad \Delta S_c = \cdot08568\,\Delta Y$

The estimate of β is practically the same as that derived from the actual values of income and savings, but the estimate of the standard error is much larger. Some light will be thrown on this phenomenon later on, when the logic of the transformation to first differences is examined.

Another modification of least-squares regression occurs when the observations represent averages of figures which are not individually given and have been grouped together. Say we have n observations, the ith observation being a mean over f_i units. Then

$$y'_i = \alpha + \beta x'_i = \bar{\epsilon}_i$$

where $\bar{\epsilon}_i$ is also a mean of f_i error terms with variance σ^2.

Taking
$$\bar{x}' = \Sigma fx'/\Sigma f$$
$$\bar{y}' = \Sigma fy'/\Sigma f$$

we have $x = x' - \bar{x}'$, $y = y' - \bar{y}'$ as before. Also

$$\Sigma fx^2 = \Sigma fx'^2 - (\Sigma fx')^2/\Sigma f$$

with corresponding expressions for Σfxy and Σfy^2. The least-squares estimator becomes

$$b = \Sigma fxy/\Sigma fx^2 \qquad (2.20)$$

Since
$$b = \beta + \Sigma fx\bar{\epsilon}/\Sigma fx^2$$
$$E(b) = \beta$$

and from
$$E(\bar{\epsilon}_i^2) = \sigma^2/f_i$$

it follows that
$$V(b) = \sigma^2/\Sigma fx^2$$

To estimate σ^2, we derive the expressions

$$\Sigma fu^2 = \Sigma fy^2 - b\Sigma fxy \qquad (2.21)$$
$$s^2 = \Sigma fu^2/(n-2) \qquad (2.22)$$

so that
$$s_b = \sqrt{s^2/\Sigma fx^2} \qquad (2.23)$$

Also
$$r^2 = b\Sigma fxy/\Sigma fy^2 \qquad (2.24)$$

and as before
$$a = \bar{y}' - b\bar{x}'$$

If the weights f attaching to the observations are equal, the formulae (2.20), (2.21) and (2.24), reduce to (2.3), (2.12) and (2.11) respectively. If formulae (2.22) and (2.23) are combined into

$$s_b = \sqrt{\Sigma fu^2/(n-2)\Sigma fx^2}$$

then in the case of equal weights also

$$s_b = \sqrt{\Sigma u^2/(n-2)\Sigma x^2}$$

15

Only the estimate s^2 is larger than that pertaining to ordinary regression, since it refers here to the error in ungrouped data which is largely concealed by grouping.

Example 2.2 Net output x' and wages plus salaries y' per establishment at the 1963 Census of Production are given as follows for 6 conurbations (in £000), together with the number of establishments f; the data were derived from the publication of the C.S.O. (1972).

	f	x'	y'
Tyneside	992	179	98
West Yorkshire	5850	81	45
Greater London	21028	91	47
West Midlands	7103	124	71
South East Lancashire	6220	112	62
Merseyside	1668	199	102

Treating each conurbation as one observation irrespective of size, the main results obtained are

$$b = \cdot5101$$
$$a = 4\cdot01$$
$$r^2 = \cdot985$$
$$s^2 = 11\cdot6$$
$$s_b = \cdot0318$$

Using weights, the calculations yield

$$\Sigma f = 42861$$
$$\Sigma fx' = 4474310$$
$$\Sigma fy' = 2408371$$
$$\Sigma fx^2 = 30515 \times 10^3$$
$$\Sigma fxy = 16780 \times 10^3$$
$$\Sigma fy^2 = 9511 \times 10^3$$
$$b = \cdot5499$$
$$a = -1\cdot20$$
$$b\Sigma fxy = 9227 \times 10^3$$
$$r^2 = \cdot970$$
$$\Sigma fu^2 = 284 \times 10^3$$
$$s^2 = 71 \times 10^3$$
$$s_b = \sqrt{\cdot002327} = \cdot0482$$

16

Thus for any additional £1000 in net output, an additional £550 appears to go on wages and salaries.

Weighted observations occur, in particular, in connection with household budget data, since results are rarely available for individual households; published data usually refer to income groups, family composition groups etc. If, however, the numbers in the various groups do not differ too much from each other, the result will often for practical purposes be the same as that obtained by using unweighted data, and this refinement may not have to be applied.

2.3 Heteroscedasticity

It is now necessary to re-examine the assumptions that have been made in deriving the least-squares estimators, and to ascertain what happens when any one of these assumptions is dropped or modified.

Firstly, the disturbances were assumed to have a probability distribution which remains the same over all observations, so that the variance in particular remains unchanged. In statistical terminology, we speak of homoscedasticity in this case and of heteroscedasticity when the assumption is discarded. In the latter case, the alternative assumption that the disturbance term is proportional to a power x'^m of x' $(0 < m \leqslant 1)$ is usually made. This state of affairs may be discovered when the residuals after regression are examined, though accurate estimation of m is difficult. If a reasonable assumption about m can be made, then the variables x' and y' may be transformed to new variables by dividing the equation by x'^m. With the new variables, the error term has the properties known in the case of homoscedasticity, and least-squares methods are applicable though they may lead to unfamiliar expressions.

If it can be assumed that the disturbance term is proportionate to x' itself, then division by x' leads to a new regression in which β becomes the constant term and α the coefficient of the independent variable. With the new variables, the optimum properties of least squares hold. Application of least squares to the original variables would still give unbiased and consistent but not best estimates, nor would the standard error formulae be strictly applicable.

In Example 2.1, it would be quite logical to assume that variations from the norm in savings tend to be proportionate to the income level, viz.

$$S = \alpha + \beta Y + \varepsilon Y$$

Hence $$S/Y = \beta + \alpha/Y + \varepsilon$$

Writing now $x' = 1/Y$, $y' = S/Y$ the equation is

$$y' = \beta + \alpha x' + \varepsilon$$

17

The data are as follows:

x'	y'	x'	y'
·0952	·0114	·0472	·0575
·0909	·0118	·0437	·0742
·0840	·0092	·0415	·0651
·0787	·0299	·0391	·0633
·0741	·0311	·0361	·0639
·0699	·0259	·0332	·0654
·0645	·0303	·0312	·0664
·0602	·0458	·0297	·0629
·0571	·0429	·0275	·0567
·0541	·0335	·0258	·0619
·0510	·0418	·0234	·0652

$$n = 22$$
$$\Sigma x' = 1·1581$$
$$\Sigma y' = 1·0161$$
$$\Sigma x^2 = ·010180$$
$$\Sigma xy = -·008751$$
$$\Sigma y^2 = ·008762$$
$$a = -·8596$$
$$b = ·09144$$

Hence the resulting equation is

$$(S/Y)_c = ·09144 - ·8596/Y$$

or
$$S_c = -·8596 + ·09144Y$$

compared with the previous result

$$S_c = -·7255 + ·08505Y$$

What the procedure comes to is that the observations with lower values of x' are given greater weight in determining the regression equation than with the use of the original variables. In this case, the earlier part of the period carries increased weight with the present method, and in these years the marginal propensity to save appears to have been somewhat higher than more recently; therefore its overall value is raised.

Exercise 2.4 In the original regression of savings on income we found that $r^2 = ·955$. Show that with the transformed data, r^2 is much lower. What do you conclude?

2.4 Autocorrelation of errors

We return now to the original assumptions underlying (2.1), and the assumption that ε_i is a variable with mean 0 and variance σ^2 is maintained. However, ε_i is now no longer assumed to be fully random, and successive values of ε_i are considered not to be statistically independent. This is the case of autocorrelation or serial correlation of errors, which may arise with time-series especially.

In this case, least-squares procedure still gives unbiased and consistent estimates, but these are not necessarily fully efficient, and the standard error formulae and significance tests do not apply, not even approximately so. To ascertain whether the errors can be regarded as random or not is therefore a matter of serious concern.

The theoretical errors ε_i are not identical with, and must not be confused with, the observed residuals after regression u_i. Nevertheless, the errors and residuals are closely related if the model is specified correctly; this is not only intuitively clear but can also be shown as follows:

$$u_i = y_i - bx_i;$$

from (2.2) and with the help of

$$b = \beta + \Sigma\, x\varepsilon / \Sigma\, x^2$$

$$u_i = (\beta - b)x_i + (\varepsilon_i - \bar{\varepsilon})$$

$$= (\varepsilon_i - \bar{\varepsilon}) - x_i \Sigma\, x\varepsilon / \Sigma x^2$$

Thus autocorrelation in ε_i will generally show up in the residuals u_i. If these are written down and an excessive bunching of positive and negative values is observed, the randomness of the errors may be queried.

A more scientific criterion is provided by the Durbin–Watson test, based on what is known as the von Neumann ratio. The basic idea is as follows. With a time-series, the observations and thus the residuals are arranged in order of time (not in order of x'). With n residuals u_i, calculate the $n-1$ differences Δu_i between successive residuals, and obtain

$$d = \Sigma\, (\Delta u)^2 / \Sigma\, u^2 \tag{2.25}$$

(in some tests, the ratio is multiplied by $n/(n-1)$ or a different factor to allow for degrees of freedom).

Now, for a random variable x_i with

19

$$E(x_i) = 0, \qquad E(x_i^2) = \sigma^2$$

we have

$$E(x_i - x_j)^2 = 2\sigma^2 \qquad (i \neq j)$$

If the residuals are random, the value of d—which must lie between 0 and 4—should be in the neighbourhood of 2. With positive auto-correlation, d will be below 2; negative autocorrelation, which is comparatively rare, will give d a value between 2 and 4. Upper and lower bounds for the critical values of d at various significance levels, by number of observations and for multiple as well as simple regression, have been derived and tabulated by Durbin and Watson (1950, 1951); extracts are reproduced in the Appendix. A similar tabulation is given by Theil and Nagar (1961).

In Example 2.1, the result was

$$y_c' = -\cdot7255 + \cdot08505x'$$

y_c'	y'	u	Δu
·17	·12	−·05	
·21	·13	−·08	−·03
·29	·11	−·18	−·10
·35	·38	·03	·21
·42	·42	·00	−·03
·49	·37	−·12	−·12
·59	·47	−·12	·00
·69	·76	·07	·19
·76	·75	−·01	−·08
·85	·62	−·23	−·22
·94	·82	−·12	·11
1·08	1·22	·14	·26
1·22	1·70	·48	·34
1·32	1·57	·25	−·23
1·45	1·62	·17	−·08
1·63	1·77	·14	−·03
1·83	1·97	·14	·00
2·00	2·13	·13	−·01
2·14	2·12	−·02	−·15
2·36	2·06	−·30	−·28
2·57	2·40	−·17	·13
2·91	2·79	−·12	·05
Sum 26·27	26·30	·03	−·07

We compute y_c', u and Δu. Note that (apart from rounding errors)

$$\Sigma y_c' = \Sigma y'$$
$$\Sigma u = 0$$
$$\Sigma \Delta u = u_n - u_1$$

which gives a check on computations. (The first two of these equalities do not hold in the case of regression without constant term.)

There is some bunching of positive and of negative residuals, and positive autocorrelation may be suspected. This is indeed confirmed by the Durbin–Watson test. We already know that

$$\Sigma u^2 = \cdot 670$$

(a slightly different result is obtained from the rounded individual values of u). Also we find that

$$\Sigma (\Delta u)^2 = \cdot 537$$
$$d = \cdot 80$$

With 22 observations, the 5 per cent significance point has the lower and upper bounds

$$d_L = 1\cdot24 \qquad d_U = 1\cdot43$$

and the 1 per cent significance point

$$d_L = 1\cdot00 \qquad d_U = 1\cdot17$$

The hypothesis of random residuals is therefore rejected. It follows that the standard error of b and confidence limits of β cannot legitimately be derived from expressions (2.13) and (2.14).

A regression equation with autocorrelated residuals is generally to be considered as unsatisfactory, and further work is required to remedy the matter; but this may be a more difficult task than detection. In some cases, an important variable influencing y' has been excluded, and multiple regression is called for; in other cases, a transformation of variables is indicated. For example, x_i' and y_i' may be replaced by new variables $x_i' - \rho x_{i-1}'$ and $y_i' - \rho y_{i-1}'$, wherein ρ represents the first order autocorrelation coefficient, or the correlation coefficient between successive values, of the errors. In order to effect the transformation, the value of ρ has to be estimated or to be assumed. Frequently it is assumed that $\rho = 1$, in which case a transformation to first differences is appropriate. In other words, a first difference transformation is called for if the differences between successive error terms can be assumed to be independently distributed sample values of a random variable.

21

Such an assumption, in the example considered here, justifies the estimation of the equation

$$\Delta S = \beta \Delta Y + \varepsilon$$

in place of the equation

$$S = \alpha + \beta Y + \varepsilon$$

If the assumption is realistic, then the estimates obtained

$$b = \cdot 08568$$
$$s_b = \cdot 0205$$

should be acceptable.

Exercise 2.5 Show that the residuals after the regression $\Delta S_c = \cdot 08568\ \Delta Y$, applied to the data derived from Example 2.1 and given in Section 2.2, show no evidence of autocorrelation.

2.5 Errors in variables

So far we have considered modifications of the error specification in (2.1). In what follows, however, the model itself becomes subject to alteration. (2.1) allows for the possibility of observational errors in the variable y', which are included in the disturbances ε_i. It does not allow for errors in the variable x'. If such errors δ_i are present, and there exists an exact relationship between the true but unobservable values ξ_i and η_i,

$$\eta_i = \alpha + \beta \xi_i$$
$$x'_i = \xi_i + \delta_i$$
$$y'_i = \eta_i + \varepsilon_i$$
$$\quad = \alpha + \beta(x'_i - \delta_i) + \varepsilon_i$$
$$y'_i = \alpha + \beta x'_i + (\varepsilon_i - \beta \delta_i) \tag{2.26}$$

The composite error terms now depend on the coefficient β which is to be estimated, and the classical assumptions do not hold. If the usual least-squares estimate, here written as b_x, is formed,

$$b_x = \Sigma\, x(\alpha + \beta x' + \varepsilon - \beta \delta)/\Sigma\, xx'$$
$$\quad = \beta(1 - \Sigma\, \delta x/\Sigma\, x^2) + \Sigma\, \varepsilon x/\Sigma\, x^2$$

Since a positive δ will raise x and a negative δ will lower x, the term $\Sigma\, \delta x/\Sigma\, x^2$ has a positive expectation; hence

$$|\, E(b_x)\,| < |\,\beta\,|$$

22

Thus b_x is biased, and the bias does not even asymptotically disappear; hence b_x does not give a consistent estimate of β in this case. Thus, the least-squares estimates are more seriously affected by errors in the independent variable than by heteroscedasticity or serial correlation in the errors of the dependent variable.

The remedy is obvious if there are no errors ε_i in the variable y. In this case, the roles of x and y may be reversed, and the second elementary regression, the regression of x on y, gives a best unbiased estimate for $1/\beta$; hence its reciprocal b_y, given by

$$b_y = \Sigma\, y^2/\Sigma\, xy \qquad (2.27)$$

yields a consistent estimate of β.

The general case provides greater difficulties. It is in practice necessary to make an assumption regarding the values of the error variances σ_δ^2 and σ_ε^2, or at least regarding their ratio. In this case, assuming normality, the maximum likelihood method is applicable and leads to the condition

$$\Sigma\,(x-X)^2/\sigma_\delta^2 + \Sigma\,(y-a-bX)^2/\sigma_\varepsilon^2 = \text{Minimum}$$

where a, b and X_i are estimates for α, β and ξ. Differentiation by X_i and setting equal to zero gives

$$(x_i - X_i)/\sigma_\delta^2 + b(y_i - a - bX_i)/\sigma_\varepsilon^2 = 0$$

$$X_i = [\sigma_\varepsilon^2\, x_i + \sigma_\delta^2\, b(y_i - a)]/(\sigma_\varepsilon^2 + b^2\, \sigma_\delta^2)$$

$$x_i - X_i = b\sigma_\delta^2(a + bx_i - y_i)/(\sigma_\varepsilon^2 + b^2\, \sigma_\delta^2)$$

$$y_i - a - bX_i = \sigma_\varepsilon^2(y_i - a - bx_i)/(\sigma_\varepsilon^2 + b^2\, \sigma_\delta^2)$$

The estimated errors in the two variables are thus perfectly correlated. Substituting these expressions, the condition becomes

$$\Sigma\,(y - a - bx)^2/(\sigma_\varepsilon^2 + b^2\, \sigma_\delta^2) = \text{Minimum}$$

Differentiation by a and b gives the conditions

$$a = 0 \qquad \text{and}$$

$$(\sigma_\varepsilon^2 + b^2\, \sigma_\delta^2)\,(b\,\Sigma\, x^2 - \Sigma\, xy) - b\,\sigma_\delta^2(b^2\,\Sigma\, x^2 - 2b\,\Sigma\, xy + \Sigma\, y^2) = 0$$

$$b^2\,\sigma_\delta^2\,\Sigma\, xy - b(\sigma_\delta^2\,\Sigma\, y^2 - \sigma_\varepsilon^2\,\Sigma\, x^2) - \sigma_\varepsilon^2\,\Sigma\, xy = 0 \qquad (2.28)$$

For $\sigma_\delta^2 = 0$ or $\sigma_\varepsilon^2 = 0$, the solution is given by the elementary regressions b_x and b_y. The general solution depends on $\sigma_\varepsilon^2/\sigma_\delta^2$; in particular, the following two cases are of interest:

23

$$\sigma_\varepsilon^2/\sigma_\delta^2 = 1$$

and
$$\sigma_\varepsilon^2/\sigma_\delta^2 = \Sigma\,y^2/\Sigma\,x^2$$

In the former case, we speak of orthogonal regression, in the latter case of diagonal regression. Indicating the solutions for b by b_o and b_d, we have

$$b_o = [(\Sigma y^2 - \Sigma x^2) + \sqrt{(\Sigma y^2 - \Sigma x^2)^2 + (2\,\Sigma xy)^2}]/2\,\Sigma xy \qquad (2.29)$$

(the negative root not being applicable) and

$$b_d = \pm\,\sqrt{\Sigma\,y^2/\Sigma\,x^2} \qquad (2.30)$$

the sign following that of $\Sigma\,xy$.

The orthogonal regression minimizes the sum of squares of the shortest distances between observations and regression line; the diagonal regression does the same when the two variables have been standardized so as to have the same variance. b_o depends on the units of measurement, and unless x' and y' are measured in the same units, it is arbitrary; this objection does not apply to b_d.

Exercise 2.6 Show that both b_o and b_d lie between b_x and b_y and thus represent compromises between the two elementary regressions.

The estimation of the ratio $\sigma_\varepsilon^2/\sigma_\delta^2$ from the data may also be attempted. This is the object, for example, of the variate difference method due to Tintner (1940).

An alternative method is that of instrumental variables, which has been chiefly developed by Reiersøl (1945) and Geary (1949). The idea is to introduce a further variable z' which is independent of the errors δ_i and ε_i, and to obtain

$$b_z = \Sigma\,yz/\Sigma\,xz \qquad (2.31)$$

Since
$$\Sigma yz = \beta\,\Sigma xz + \Sigma\,\varepsilon z - \beta\,\Sigma\,\delta z$$
$$b_z = \beta + (\Sigma\,\varepsilon z - \beta\,\Sigma\,\delta z)/\Sigma xz$$

The estimator is clearly unbiased and consistent. It cannot, of course, be expected to have minimum sampling variance.

In practice, it is not always easy to find a suitable instrumental variable, and there is an element of arbitrariness in it. To be useful, the instrumental variable must be highly correlated with both x' and y', as otherwise no reasonably accurate estimation would be possible.

Example 2.3 From data given by the O.E.C.D. (1966), the average annual percentage increase between 1950 and 1965 in real gross national product (x'), employment (y') and real gross fixed investment (z') is obtained for thirteen countries, as follows:

Country	x'	y'	z'
Austria	5·2	·2	7·5
Canada	4·5	2·1	4·7
Denmark	3·9	·9	7·0
France	4·7	·2	5·6
Germany (F.R.)	6·8	1·7	9·1
Ireland	2·4	−1·0	5·0
Italy	5·5	1·0	7·0
Japan	10·4	2·5	13·6
Netherlands	4·8	1·1	6·1
Norway	4·0	·3	4·5
Switzerland	4·7	1·8	8·8
United Kingdom	2·9	·7	5·6
United States	3·7	1·4	2·8

The data are used to estimate the change in employment which is associated with an increase in gross national product. As both variables may be subject to error, both elementary regressions and the two weighted regressions are to be computed, as well as the regression with investment as instrumental variable. The usual computations give

$$\Sigma x^2 = 48·057$$
$$\Sigma xy = 14·738$$
$$\Sigma y^2 = 10·629$$

and also

$$\Sigma xz = 56·403$$
$$\Sigma yz = 15·372$$

Hence

$$b_x = 14·738/48·057 = ·3067$$
$$b_y = 10·629/14·738 = ·7212$$
$$b_o = (-37·428 + \sqrt{37·438^2 + 29·476^2})/29·476$$
$$= (-37·428 + 47·641)/29·476 = ·3465$$
$$b_d = \sqrt{·221\,175} = ·4703$$
$$b_z = 15·372/56·403 = ·2725$$

The five estimates for β differ substantially from each other, ranging from ·27 to ·72. The orthogonal and instrumental variables regressions come out close to the first elementary regression, whilst the second elementary regression is quite different. If errors of measurement in x' are really important, then there is considerable uncertainty regarding the numerical effect of output growth on employment.

Estimates for the constant term vary similarly: since

$$\Sigma x' = 63 \cdot 5$$
$$\Sigma y' = 12 \cdot 9$$
$$a = (12 \cdot 9 - 63 \cdot 5b)/13$$
$$a_x = - \cdot 506$$
$$a_y = -2 \cdot 530$$
$$a_o = - \cdot 700$$
$$a_d = -1 \cdot 305$$
$$a_z = - \cdot 339$$

α represents the annual percentage change in employment which would be associated with real gross national product remaining constant. All estimates of α indicate a decline in employment in these circumstances, but this may lie between less than $\frac{1}{2}$ per cent on one hand and $2\frac{1}{2}$ per cent on the other.

Generally errors of measurement are considered to be negligible in comparison with errors in equations. If it were not so, ordinary least squares would frequently have to be rejected, and the econometrician would be faced with even greater estimation difficulties than is the case at present.

2.1 From (2.5) and well-known formulae for arithmetic progressions:

$$\Sigma x^2 = n(n+1)(2n+1)/6 - [n(n+1)/2]^2/n$$
$$= n(n+1)(n-1)/12 = (n^3-n)/12$$

Thus from (2.8)

$$V(b) = 12\sigma^2/(n^3-n)$$

On the other hand,

$$\bar{x}'_3 - \bar{x}'_1 = 2n/3$$

and by (2.10)

$$V(b'') = 27\sigma^2/2n^3$$
$$\sim 9V(b)/8$$

2.2
$$\Delta y'_n = \cdot 28$$
$$\Delta b' = \cdot 28/32 \cdot 3 = \cdot 008\,67$$
$$\Delta b'' = \cdot 28/152 \cdot 5 = \cdot 001\,84$$
$$\Delta b = \cdot 28\,(42 \cdot 8 - 496 \cdot 9/22)/1950 \cdot 6$$
$$= 5 \cdot 6598/1950 \cdot 6 = \cdot 002\,90$$
$$\Delta b'/b' = \cdot 105$$
$$\Delta b''/b'' = \cdot 021$$
$$\Delta b/b = \cdot 034$$

2.3
$$\Sigma x' = 253$$
$$\Sigma x^2 = 885 \cdot 5$$
$$\Sigma xy = 414 \cdot 32 - 253 \times 26 \cdot 30/22$$
$$= 111 \cdot 87$$
$$b = \cdot 126\,34$$
$$r^2 = 14 \cdot 134/14 \cdot 779 = \cdot 956$$

2.4
$$r^2 = \cdot 8596 \times \cdot 008\,751/\cdot 008\,762$$
$$= \cdot 859$$

This does not mean that the new regression is inferior to the one previously obtained. The savings ratio varies relatively less than savings, and there is less to explain in the transformed than in the original equation.

27

2.5	ΔS_c	u	Δu
	·04	− ·03	
	·08	− ·10	− ·07
	·07	·20	·30
	·07	− ·03	− ·23
	·07	− ·12	− ·09
	·10	·00	·12
	·09	·20	·20
	·08	− ·09	− ·29
	·09	− ·22	− ·13
	·09	·11	·33
	·14	·26	·15
	·15	·33	·07
	·10	− ·23	− ·56
	·13	− ·08	·15
	·18	− ·03	·05
	·21	− ·01	·02
	·17	− ·01	·00
	·14	− ·15	− ·14
	·22	− ·28	− ·13
	·21	·13	·41
	·34	·05	− ·08

$\Sigma u^2 = \cdot 5315$ (or ·5320 from rounded values above)

$\Sigma (\Delta u)^2 = \cdot 9976$

$d = 1 \cdot 88$ which is close to 2

2.6
$$b_d = \sqrt{b_x \, b_y}$$
From (2.18),
$$b_o(b_o \, \Sigma \, xy - \Sigma \, y^2) + (b_o \, \Sigma \, x^2 - \Sigma \, xy) = 0$$
$$\Sigma \, xy = b_x \, \Sigma \, x^2$$
$$\Sigma \, y^2 = b_y \, \Sigma \, xy$$
$$b_o \, \Sigma \, xy(b_o - b_y) + \Sigma \, x^2 \, (b_o - b_x) = 0$$
Since $b_o \, \Sigma \, xy > 0$, $b_o - b_y$ and $b_o - b_x$ must have opposite signs.

28

3. MULTIPLE REGRESSION

3.1 Classical theory

In many instances, a simple regression on a single variable is not acceptable. There may be *a priori* theoretical or empirical reasons for this—the latter, for example, being a poor fit, or non-randomness of residuals. If theoretical considerations demand it or if the unsatisfactory results cannot be improved by a transformation of variables, two or more explanatory variables have to be introduced. Sometimes terms of higher order in one or several variables, like x_1^2 or $x_1 x_2$, are introduced; these are treated as new variables.

The assumptions made here are analogous to the case of simple regression. A linear relationship is assumed, if necessary after transformation of variables; such a transformation may also be made to secure homoscedasticity of errors. The explanatory variables are assumed to be observed without error, and the error in the equation is taken as a random variable with mean 0 and variance σ^2.

Suppose we are given k explanatory variables $x_1', \ldots, x_k'$ $(k \geqslant 2)$ and the dependent variable y' which is to be explained. For simplicity's sake, the analysis which follows deals with the deviations from their means $x_1, \ldots, x_k$ and y. The relationship then is

$$y_i = \beta_1 x_{1i} + \cdots + \beta_k x_{ki} + (\varepsilon_i - \bar{\varepsilon}) \qquad (i = 1, \ldots, n) \qquad (3.1)$$

The classical method of least squares is then applicable and yields a maximum-likelihood estimate under the assumption of normality, and in any case best unbiased estimators for the regression coefficients. The estimates $b_1, \ldots, b_k$ for $\beta_1, \ldots, \beta_k$ satisfy the condition that

$$\Sigma (y - b_1 x_1 - \cdots - b_k x_k)^2 = \text{Minimum}$$

which yields the k equations

$$\left.\begin{aligned}
b_1 \Sigma x_1^2 + \cdots + b_k \Sigma x_1 x_k &= \Sigma x_1 y \\
\cdots \cdots \cdots \cdots \cdots \cdots \cdots \\
b_1 \Sigma x_k x_1 + \cdots + b_k \Sigma x_k^2 &= \Sigma x_k y
\end{aligned}\right\} \qquad (3.2)$$

The solution may be written as

$$b_i = (A_{i1} \Sigma x_1 y + \cdots + A_{ik} \Sigma x_k y)/D \qquad (3.3)$$

where D is the determinant

$$D = \begin{vmatrix} \Sigma x_1^2 \ldots \Sigma x_1 x_k \\ \cdot \cdot \cdot \cdot \cdot \cdot \cdot \\ \Sigma x_k x_1 \ldots \Sigma x_k^2 \end{vmatrix} \qquad (3.4)$$

and A_{ik} is the co-factor of $\Sigma x_i x_k$ in D.

With the help of (3.1) and the well-known property of determinants that

$$A_{i1} \Sigma x_j x_1 + \dots + A_{ik} \Sigma x_j x_k = \begin{cases} D & i = j \\ 0 & i \neq j \end{cases}$$

we obtain

$$b_i = \beta_i + (A_{i1} \Sigma \varepsilon x_1 + \dots + A_{ik} \Sigma \varepsilon x_k)/D \qquad (3.5)$$

Hence $\qquad E(b_i) = \beta_i$

and with the help of the same property it follows that

$$V(b_i) = A_{ii} D\sigma^2/D^2$$

$$V(b_i) = \sigma^2 A_{ii}/D \qquad (3.6)$$

From the sum of squares of residuals which is computed with the formula

$$\Sigma u^2 = \Sigma y^2 - (b_1 \Sigma x_1 y + \dots + b_k \Sigma x_k y) \qquad (3.7)$$

an unbiased estimate of σ^2 is obtained in

$$s^2 = \Sigma u^2/(n-k-1) \qquad (3.8)$$

and thus the standard errors of the regression coefficients are estimated as

$$s_{bi} = \sqrt{s^2 A_{ii}/D} \qquad (3.9)$$

For $k = 2$, formulae (3.3), (3.6) and (3.9) simplify since

$$D = \Sigma x_1^2 \Sigma x_2^2 - (\Sigma x_1 x_2)^2$$

$$A_{11} = \Sigma x_2^2, \qquad A_{22} = \Sigma x_1^2$$

$$A_{12} = A_{21} = -\Sigma x_1 x_2$$

The estimate s^2 has $n-k-1$ degrees of freedom, and accordingly, the appropriate t-distribution is used in constructing confidence intervals for β_i and in applying significance tests to b_i. In particular, the significance of the difference between b_i and 0 may be tested, and if this is not significant, the variable x_i may be omitted, though this is not and should not be automatically done if there are good theoretical reasons for retaining the variable.

The coefficient of multiple determination R^2 is also computed as follows:

$$\left. \begin{aligned} R^2 &= (b_1 \Sigma x_1 y + \dots + b_k \Sigma x_k y)/\Sigma y^2 \\ &= 1 - \Sigma u^2/\Sigma y^2 \end{aligned} \right\} \qquad (3.10)$$

Its significance, and hence the overall significance of the regression, is tested by analysis of variance, and thus by obtaining the ratio

$$\left. \begin{aligned} F &= (n-k-1)R^2/k\,(1-R^2) \\ &= (n-k-1)\,(\Sigma\,y^2 - \Sigma\,u^2)/k\,\Sigma\,u^2 \end{aligned} \right\} \qquad (3.11)$$

and testing it against the F-distribution with k and $n-k-1$ degrees of freedom.

Sometimes, a coefficient of determination $\bar{R}^2$ adjusted for degrees of freedom, in analogy with s^2, is computed in place of R^2. Whilst in accordance with (3.10)

$$1 - R^2 = \Sigma u^2/\Sigma y^2$$

$\bar{R}^2$ is defined by the relationship

$$\left. \begin{aligned} 1 - \bar{R}^2 &= (n-1)\,\Sigma u^2/(n-k-1)\,\Sigma y^2 \\ &= (n-1)(1-R^2)/(n-k-1) \end{aligned} \right\} \qquad (3.12)$$

Obviously $\qquad\qquad\qquad 1 - \bar{R}^2 > 1 - R^2$

hence $\qquad\qquad\qquad\qquad \bar{R}^2 < R^2$

Returning to the original variables $x'_1, \ldots, x'_k$ and y', the constant term is

$$a = [\Sigma y' - (b_1 \Sigma x'_1 + \ldots + b_k \Sigma x'_k)]/n \qquad (3.13)$$

These are the most important calculations; other statistics like the partial correlation coefficients may be defined and derived, but they are of lesser importance. The Durbin–Watson d-statistic may be used to test for randomness of the residuals; other variables may be brought in if the assumption of randomness cannot be maintained.

Example 3.1 Household expenditure on food in Ireland is taken as a linear function of total household expenditure and household size. The observations are averages for sixteen size/income groups in a household budget enquiry, published by the Irish C.S.O. (1969).

Total expenditure (£ per week) x'_1	Number of persons x'_2	Food expenditure (£ per week) y'
6·85	1·42	2·72
14·75	1·81	4·40
23·39	1·84	5·40
34·28	1·90	6·74
10·74	3·31	4·58 (contd.)

31

	18·04	3·48	6·16
	25·51	3·55	7·48
	37·30	3·62	8·84
	12·34	5·31	5·83
	18·24	5·45	7·09
	26·74	5·42	8·70
	40·12	5·45	10·45
	10·83	7·40	5·64
	19·12	8·33	8·31
	27·15	8·84	10·28
	41·88	8·63	12·88
Sum	367·28	75·76	115·50

Computation and some rounding-off yields

$$\Sigma x_1^2 = 10\,253\cdot0702 - 8430\cdot9124 = 1822\cdot16$$
$$\Sigma x_1 x_2 = 1837\cdot8694 - 1739\cdot0708 = 98\cdot80$$
$$\Sigma x_2^2 = 454\cdot8104 - 358\cdot7236 = 96\cdot09$$
$$\Sigma x_1 y = 3013\cdot3882 - 2651\cdot3025 = 362\cdot09$$
$$\Sigma x_2 y = 616\cdot4120 - 546\cdot8925 = 69\cdot52$$
$$\Sigma y^2 = 935\cdot9520 - 833\cdot7656 = 102\cdot19$$
$$D = 1822\cdot16 \times 96\cdot09 - (98\cdot80)^2 = 165\,330$$
$$b_1 = (96\cdot09 \times 362\cdot09 - 98\cdot80 \times 69\cdot52)/165\,330$$
$$= \cdot168\,90$$
$$b_2 = (1822\cdot16 \times 69\cdot52 - 98\cdot80 \times 362\cdot09)/165\,330$$
$$= \cdot549\,82$$
$$a = (115\cdot50 - \cdot168\,90 \times 367\cdot28 - 549\,82 \times 75\cdot76)/16$$
$$= \cdot7383$$

Therefore the estimated relationship is

$$y_c' = \cdot7383 + \cdot168\,90\, x_1' + \cdot549\,82\, x_2'$$

It tells us that about one-sixth of any additional household expenditure goes on food, compared with an average proportion of almost one-third $(115\cdot50/367\cdot28 = \cdot314)$. With given total expenditure, an increase in household size involves an additional food expenditure of 55 pence per additional person, to be offset by reduced spending on other items.

Furthermore

$$b_1 \Sigma x_1 y + b_2 \Sigma x_2 y = 99 \cdot 38$$
$$R^2 = 99 \cdot 38 / 102 \cdot 19 = \cdot 973$$
$$\bar{R}^2 = 1 - 15(1 - \cdot 973)/13 = \cdot 969$$

The fit of the equation to the data is very good, and it is hardly necessary to test the overall significance of the regression. Also

$$\Sigma u^2 = 102 \cdot 19 - 99 \cdot 38 = 2 \cdot 81$$
$$s^2 = 2 \cdot 81/13 = \cdot 2162$$
$$s_{b_1} = \sqrt{\cdot 2162 \times 96 \cdot 09 / 165\,330}$$
$$= \sqrt{\cdot 000\,2566} = \cdot 0160$$
$$s_{b_2} = \sqrt{\cdot 2162 \times 1822 \cdot 16 / 165\,330}$$
$$= \sqrt{\cdot 002\,3828} = \cdot 0488$$

It is not difficult to see that both regression coefficients are highly significant. Clearly both variables should be retained in the regression.

Exercise 3.1 Compare the result and the fit with those obtained by simple regression of food expenditure on total expenditure, and comment.

3.2 Multicollinearity

Difficulties arise when the explanatory variables are highly correlated between themselves, and one of them could well be expressed as a linear function of the others. In such a case we speak of multicollinearity. What happens then is that the partial regression coefficients become very sensitive to errors, and their estimation becomes impracticable.

The presence of multicollinearity is sometimes detected by high standard errors of the regression coefficients, which thus become not significant; but this is not invariably the case. Frisch (1934) showed that highly inaccurate results may be obtained without their inaccuracy being shown up by the standard errors, and he therefore recommended a systematic approach to the problem through what is known as confluence analysis or bunch map analysis.

The basic idea of this technique is to estimate all possible regressions between the variables which are considered as relevant in the investigated relationship, taking each variable successively as the dependent variable and considering all possible subsets as well as the full set of variables. In this approach, the original dependent variable, which is definitely to be included, is generally denoted by x_1 rather than by y, and there is full symmetry between the variables. The effect of adding or dropping a variable upon the partial regression coefficients and coefficients of determination may then be judged, and according to their effect a variable is classified as useful, superfluous, or detrimental.

Broadly speaking, a variable is considered as useful if its addition substantially increases the value of R^2. If it does not and its addition leaves the remaining regression coefficients largely unchanged, it is described as superfluous; generally the regression coefficient on a superfluous variable is small and insignificant. If the addition of the variable substantially changes all estimates of regression coefficients without noticeably improving the fit, it is taken to be detrimental.

With the addition of a superfluous or detrimental variable, the value of $\bar{R}^2$ may actually decline; this does not apply to R^2.

Bunch map analysis, which uses graphical methods, has been applied in some econometric investigations, notably those of Stone (1945, 1954a). Extensive computations are involved with a large number of variables. The analysis seems appropriate if it is assumed that the errors are chiefly errors of measurement in variables and appear in more than one variable. It has been shown in the case of one explanatory variable that the first elementary regression does not necessarily give the best estimates in these circumstances. With multiple regression, it similarly appears a suitable procedure to consider all the elementary regressions together with possible compromise solutions.

If the choice of the dependent variable appears clear on theoretical grounds and if errors are assumed to be additive terms in the equation rather than measurement errors, it seems more logical to consider only the regression of one dependent variable on the others; but it will generally be worthwhile to study subsets of variables as well as the full set, as the correct specification of the equation is often in doubt.

If the presence of multicollinearity has been established, it is not always easy to remedy this state of affairs. If a detrimental variable is omitted to obtain more reliable results for the other variables, this omission must be borne in mind when interpreting the results. It cannot be said that the omitted variable has no effect but merely that its effect is confounded with that of the other explanatory variables and cannot be isolated.

In some cases, restrictions on the values of the parameters may be introduced on *a priori* grounds; for example, two parameters may be set equal, or their sum may be taken to have a fixed value. In other cases, an empirically obtained value may be inserted into an equation;

34

the classical example is the insertion of cross-section results into equations using time-series. In any event, a procedure of this kind means a smaller number of regression coefficients which are to be estimated.

Multicollinearity is serious when emphasis lies on the estimation of individual parameters in the relationship, but less serious when the objective of prediction for the dependent variable is stressed; for the latter purpose, even a simple regression may often suffice if the relationship between the explanatory variables is approximately maintained. It is even held by some writers that prediction is all that matters, and thus simple regression should be used whenever possible. This point has been most forcefully expressed by Geary (1963), who also holds that the regression coefficients are meaningful only in simple regression or with orthogonal variables.

Example 3.2 A production function for British industry is to be constructed on the basis of data for labour, capital and output at 5-year intervals between 1871 and 1911. The data are taken from a paper by Phelps Brown and Handfield-Jones (1952), and the regressions derived here represent a partial and simplified version of a study by Leser (1954). The data have the following meaning:

L: operatives in industry covered by Hoffman's index (millions),
K: capital at 1912–13 prices excluding houses (£ mill.),
P: Hoffman's index of industrial production (1890–99 = 100),

and the data themselves, together with their logarithms to which they were transformed before applying the regression, are given in the following table. x_1' was obtained for non-Census years by interpolation.

Year	L	K	P	$\log_{10}L$ $= x_1'$	$\log_{10}K$ $= x_2'$	$\log_{10}P-1$ $= y'$
1871	2·647	1·747	68	·423	·242	·832
1876		1·994	73	·447	·300	·863
1881	2·961	2·214	81	·471	·345	·908
1886		2·438	81	·503	·387	·908
1891	3·428	2·773	97	·535	·443	·987
1896		3·098	104	·564	·491	1·017
1901	3·916	3·698	111	·593	·568	1·045
1906		4·245	124	·631	·628	1·093
1911	4·668	4·662	130	·669	·669	1·114
				4·836	4·073	8·767

$$\Sigma\, x_1^2 = 2\cdot655280 - 2\cdot598544 = \cdot056736$$
$$\Sigma\, x_1 x_2 = 2\cdot288204 - 2\cdot188559 = \cdot099645$$
$$\Sigma\, x_2^2 = 2\cdot019257 - 1\cdot843259 = \cdot175998$$
$$\Sigma\, x_1 y = 4\cdot778356 - 4\cdot710801 = \cdot067555$$
$$\Sigma\, x_2 y = 4\cdot086718 - 3\cdot967555 = \cdot119163$$
$$\Sigma\, y^2 = 8\cdot622049 - 8\cdot540032 = \cdot082017$$

Only the coefficients b_i, not the constant term a, are of interest. Simple regression of y' on x_1' gives

$$b_1 = \cdot067555/\cdot056736 = 1\cdot191$$
$$b_1\,\Sigma\, x_1 y = \cdot080458$$
$$r^2 = \cdot080458/\cdot082017 = \cdot9810$$

and simple regression on x_2':

$$b_2 = \cdot119163/\cdot175998 = \cdot677$$
$$b_2\,\Sigma\, x_2 y = \cdot080673$$
$$r^2 = \cdot080673/\cdot082017 = \cdot9836$$

Multiple regression yields

$$D = \cdot056736 \times \cdot175998 - \cdot099645^2 = 56\cdot30 \times 10^{-6}$$
$$b_1 = (\cdot175998 \times \cdot067555 - \cdot099645 \times \cdot119163)/D$$
$$= 15\cdot55/56\cdot30 = \cdot276$$
$$b_2 = (\cdot056736 \times \cdot119163 - \cdot099645 \times \cdot067555)/D$$
$$= 29\cdot31/56\cdot30 = \cdot521$$
$$b_1\,\Sigma\, x_1 y + b_2\,\Sigma\, x_2 y = \cdot080729$$
$$R^2 = \cdot080729/\cdot082017 = \cdot9843$$

Thus the addition of x_1' hardly improves the fit compared with the simple regression on x_2', whilst b_2 is changed from $\cdot677$ to $\cdot521$; the addition of x_2' also does little to improve the simple regression on x_1', whilst b_1 is changed from $1\cdot191$ to $\cdot276$. Multicollinearity is thus suspected.

It can also be seen that possible errors in the variables exert a strong influence on the results. This is seen most easily when an error in y is considered.

Exercise 3.2 If for 1871, P was changed to 69 and thus y' to $\cdot839$, how would b_1 and b_2 be affected?

This sensitivity to errors is also shown up here by high standard errors, since

$$\Sigma u^2 = \cdot082017 - \cdot080729 = \cdot001288$$
$$s^2 = \cdot001288/6 = \cdot0002147$$
$$s_{b1} = \sqrt{\cdot0002147 \times \cdot175998/\cdot0000563}$$
$$= \sqrt{\cdot6712} = \cdot819$$
$$s_{b2} = \sqrt{\cdot0002147 \times \cdot056736/\cdot0000563}$$
$$= \sqrt{\cdot2164} = \cdot465$$

It is therefore quite clear that the estimates b_1 and b_2 are unreliable.

In this instance there are good theoretical grounds for believing that in the relationship

$$\log P = \alpha + \beta_1 \log L + \beta_2 \log K$$

β_1 and β_2 are not independent, but that on the contrary

$$\beta_1 + \beta_2 = 1$$

so that the relationship may be written, for example, by putting $\beta = \beta_2$:

$$\log P = \alpha + (1 - \beta) \log L + \beta \log K$$
$$\log P/L = \alpha + \beta \log K/L$$

and an estimate b may be obtained by simple regression between the following new variables:

$\log_{10} K/L + 1$ $= x'$	$\log_{10} P/L - 1$ $= y'$
$\cdot819$	$\cdot409$
$\cdot853$	$\cdot416$
$\cdot874$	$\cdot437$
$\cdot884$	$\cdot405$
$\cdot908$	$\cdot452$
$\cdot927$	$\cdot453$
$\cdot975$	$\cdot452$
$\cdot997$	$\cdot462$
$1\cdot000$	$\cdot445$
$8\cdot237$	$3\cdot931$

With the new variables,

$$\Sigma x^2 = 7\cdot572129 - 7\cdot538685 = \cdot033444$$
$$\Sigma xy = 3\cdot606438 - 3\cdot597739 = \cdot008699$$
$$\Sigma y^2 = 1\cdot720617 - 1\cdot716973 = \cdot003644$$
$$b = \cdot260$$
$$b\Sigma xy = \cdot002262$$
$$R^2 = \cdot621$$

Exercise 3.3 Show that these results could also have been derived from the sums of squares and cross-products of the original variables without explicitly obtaining the new variables.

The value of R^2, which seems low, is of course not comparable to R^2 obtained for the original variables since $\Sigma\, y^2$ is now much lower than before. If a comparison is required, we compute

$$R'^2 = 1 - \Sigma\, u^2 / \Sigma\, y^2$$

where $\Sigma\, y^2$ refers to the original variable $\log P$. Then

$$\Sigma\, u^2 = \cdot003644 - \cdot002262 = \cdot001382$$
$$R'^2 = 1 - \cdot001382/\cdot082017 = \cdot9831$$

which is little below the value of $\cdot9843$ obtained by multiple regression. Furthermore,

$$s^2 = \cdot001382/7 = \cdot0001974$$
$$s_b = \sqrt{\cdot0001974/\cdot033444} = \sqrt{\cdot005902}$$
$$= \cdot0768$$

Thus under these assumptions the estimated relationship is

$$\log P = \text{const.} + \cdot740 \log L + \cdot260 \log K$$

both coefficients having an estimated standard error of $\cdot077$. This result might be acceptable, though it will be seen later in discussing production functions that alternative interpretations are possible.

3.3 Time as a variable

Time as measured by the number of observation periods from a starting value onward may be explicitly introduced into the equations when dealing with time-series. Even when the other variables are subjected to a logarithmic or other transformation, time is usually introduced as a linear term, as its origin is arbitrary, and with a transformed value the resulting regression coefficients would also be arbitrary. Sometimes, however, quadratic and higher order terms in time are introduced besides linear terms.

The implicit assumption is that the constant term in the equation increases or decreases steadily, but that the coefficients of the other variables remain unaltered. It is easy to modify this assumption; if it is believed that the coefficient of x_i is subject to long-term changes, a term with tx_i (t denoting time) may be introduced into the equation as an additional variable, and the significance of its regression coefficient may be tested.

The introduction of time as a variable comes to the same as regressing each variable $x_1, \ldots, x_{k-1}, y$ on time x_k, obtaining the deviations $x_1^*, \ldots, x_{k-1}^*, y^*$ from the regression, and regressing y^* on $x_1^*, \ldots, x_{k-1}^*$.

This is easily seen for $k = 2$, since then

$$x_1^* = x_1 - x_2 \Sigma x_1 x_2 / \Sigma x_2^2$$
$$y^* = y - x_2 \Sigma x_2 y / \Sigma x_2^2$$
$$\Sigma x_1^{*2} = \Sigma x_1^2 - (\Sigma x_1 x_2)^2 / \Sigma x_2^2$$
$$\Sigma x_1^* y^* = \Sigma x_1 y - \Sigma x_1 x_2 \Sigma x_2 y / \Sigma x_2^2$$
$$\Sigma x_1^* y^* / \Sigma x_1^{*2} = (\Sigma x_2^2 \Sigma x_1 y - \Sigma x_1 x_2 \Sigma x_2 y) / [\Sigma x_1^2 \Sigma x_2^2 - (\Sigma x_1 x_2)^2]$$

which from (3.3) is the estimate for b_1 in the regression of y on x_1 and x_2.

Exercise 3.4 Generalize this result to $k > 2$ variables.

Another favourite device in time-series is to use first differences between successive terms, instead of the original variables and time. The exact theoretical relationship is the same in both cases; for

$$y_t' = \alpha + \beta_1 x_{1,t}' + \ldots + \beta_{k-1} x_{k-1,t}' + \beta_k x_{k,t}'$$
$$y_{t-1}' = \alpha + \beta_1 x_{1,t-1}' + \ldots + \beta_{k-1} x_{k-1,t-1}' + \beta_k x_{k,t-1}'$$

where x_k' is time, so that

$$x_{k,t}' = x_{k,t-1}' + 1$$

Then $y_t' - y_{t-1}'$

$$= \beta_k + \beta_1 (x_{1,t}' - x_{1,t-1}') + \ldots + \beta_{k-1} (x_{k-1,t}' - x_{k-1,t-1}')$$

But the error specification is different; in this approach the errors in the original variables are assumed to be autocorrelated in such a manner that the errors in the first differences are random. Thus estimation from first differences generally leads to different results for the coefficients as compared with estimation from original variables. It may reduce a multiple to a simple regression.

Exercise 3.5 Using the data for $x_1' = \log K/L + 1$ and $y' = \log P/L - 1$ in Example 3.2, construct the partial regression of y' on x_1' and $x_2' =$ time. Also construct the regression between first differences in $\log K/L$ and $\log P/L$, and compare.

The use of first differences offers great advantages, as the implied error specification is less rigid and in many instances more realistic than that implied by using the original data. There is also less danger in uncritically accepting a result on the basis of a high coefficient of determination in this case. This danger is always present when a number of time-series which exhibit a common upward trend are related to each other; it has been specially pointed out by Yule (1926).

On the other hand, the introduction of time, whether explicitly as a variable or implicitly as a constant term with first differences, is not invariably a satisfying procedure on theoretical grounds. In some cases, the coefficient can be naturally interpreted as an autonomous growth, but in other cases it merely represents the combined effect of a number of unspecified factors. If it is possible to specify some of these factors and explicitly introduce them into the regression so that the contribution of unspecified factors to the explanation becomes small or negligible this will obviously be preferable.

A different way altogether in which time may be said to enter a relationship is through lagged variables. There is of course no difficulty whatever in introducing a variable referring to a previous period if the variable for the current period does not enter the relationship. The case where both unlagged and lagged values of a variable appear, which may arise in a system of simultaneous equations, demands special consideration. There are often good theoretical grounds for assuming a fixed or distributed time-lag in the relationship, and the use of lags is a legitimate device in regression analysis.

To ascertain the most suitable lag or lag structure may call for considerable computational effort, but this can be much reduced by making simplifying assumptions. Following Koyck (1954), the effect of a lagged variable may be assumed to decline in geometric progression with the length of a lag, at least from some point on. In the simplest case,

$$y' = \alpha + \beta(x' + \lambda x'_{-1} + \lambda^2 x'_{-2} + \ldots) + \varepsilon$$

Then
$$y'_{-1} = \alpha + \beta(x'_{-1} + \lambda x'_{-2} + \ldots) + \varepsilon_{-1}$$

and
$$y' = (1-\lambda)\alpha + \beta x' + \lambda y'_{-1} + (\varepsilon - \lambda\varepsilon_{-1})$$

so that a regression with two independent variables only is involved.

A word of caution should, however, be added here. With auto-correlated errors, the use of lagged values of the dependent variable as explanatory variables leads to bias in the same way as errors in the independent variable do in simple regression. This may also apply to the Koyck model; and lagged variables may thus lead to difficult econometric problems.

3.4 Dummy variables and parallel regressions

It frequently happens that the dependent variable in a regression equation is influenced not only by several other variables but also by the presence or absence of an attribute, or by a characteristic for which a number of non-quantifiable alternatives are possible. In these circumstances, a dummy variable, or several dummy variables, assuming the values 0 and 1 only, may be introduced into the equation. Generally, the assumption is implicitly made that these qualitative factors induce a shift in the regression equation but leave the coefficients of the other variables unchanged.

For example, if the data are time series extending over both war-time and peace-time years, it may be felt that war-time conditions exert an influence upon the dependent variable which operates as an additive influence. In this case, a dummy variable which has the value 0 for peace-time years and 1 for war-time years may be used; its coefficient will then show the effect of war conditions.

When there are m alternatives, then $m-1$ dummy variables are required. For example, when using quarterly data which are subject to seasonal influences and have not been seasonally corrected, then three dummy variables are introduced into the equation. They may, for example, assume the value 1 in the second, third and fourth quarter respectively, whilst being equal to 0 in the remaining three quarters.

With several dummy variables, the choice is to some extent arbitrary. As far as the estimated equation is concerned, the choice does not matter, but it influences the result of the significance tests applied to the coefficients of the dummy variables, and this is of some importance when some of the dummy variables are being considered for elimination.

For example, with five social classes $A-E$, the following schemes may be adopted for the dummy variables d_1, d_2, d_3, and d_4:

	d_1	d_2	d_3	d_4
A	0	0	0	0
B	1	0	0	0
C	0	1	0	0
D	0	0	1	0
E	0	0	0	1

In this case, the dummy variables show the differences between social class A on one hand and each of the other classes on the other. But instead, the dummy variables may be chosen as follows:

	d_1	d_2	d_3	d_4
A	0	0	0	0
B	1	0	0	0
C	1	1	0	0
D	1	1	1	0
E	1	1	1	1

in which case they describe the differences between A and B, B and C, C and D, D and E respectively. This may be a better idea if the classes are arranged in ascending or descending order, and if amalgamation of two or more classes is being considered.

41

Dummy variables involve easier computations than an equal number of ordinary variables; all the same, several dummies in addition to at least one ordinary variable may involve an appreciable computational burden. This does not matter when calculations can be done on an automatic computer, but when using a desk computer, the consideration may be quite a serious one.

An alternative method which leads to virtually the same result is that of parallel regression. The basic idea consists in specifying that the regression equation is the same for each of the m groups which are distinguished except for the constant term which may vary from group to group. This implies the use of deviations from the group means, instead of deviations from an overall mean, in computing the sums of squares and cross products for the ordinary variables. In the simplest case, with only one independent variable of this kind, and n_i observations in each of the m groups, the least squares condition leads to the formulae

$$b = \Sigma_i\Sigma_j(x'_{ij}-\bar{x}'_i)(y'_{ij}-\bar{y}'_i)/\Sigma_i\Sigma_j(x'_{ij}-\bar{x}'_i)^2 \qquad (3.14)$$

and $$a_i = (\Sigma_j y'_{ij}-b\Sigma_j x'_{ij})/n_i \qquad (3.15)$$

where x'_{ij}, y'_{ij} represents the jth observation in the ith group and $\bar{x}'_i$, $\bar{y}'_i$ the ith group mean.

This procedure does not lead to a significance test for the difference between the constant terms in pairs of groups, but instead the overall significance of differences between the constant terms may be tested by means of an analysis of variance. If the differences are found to be not significant, an ordinary least squares regression may be computed. Analysis of variance may also be used to investigate the possibility that entirely separate regressions are required for each group.

In Example 3.1, instead of introducing number of persons into the regression, household size could be allowed for by three dummy variables, or by a regression with four different constant terms. Choosing the latter way, we have four groups with four observations each, and we write

Group	$\Sigma x'$	$\Sigma y'$	$\Sigma x'^2$	$\Sigma x'y'$	$\Sigma y'^2$
1	79·27	19·26	1986·6955	440·8852	101·3460
2	91·59	27·06	2482·8393	680·8624	193·0180
3	97·44	32·07	2809·6152	853·1558	269·1495
4	98·98	37·11	2973·9202	1038·4848	372·4385
Sum	367·28	115·50	10253·0702	3013·3882	935·9520

checking the column totals against the previously obtained results.

Then, for example, for the first group

$$\Sigma(x' - \bar{x}_1')^2 = 1986 \cdot 6955 - 79 \cdot 27^2/4$$
$$= 415 \cdot 762$$
$$\Sigma(x' - \bar{x}_1')(y' - \bar{y}_1') = 440 \cdot 8852 - 79 \cdot 27 \times 19 \cdot 26/4$$
$$= 59 \cdot 200$$
$$\Sigma(y' - \bar{y}_1')^2 = 101 \cdot 3460 - 19 \cdot 26^2/4$$
$$= 8 \cdot 609$$

If this is done for all groups, the results are:

Group	$\Sigma(x' - \bar{x}_i')^2$	$\Sigma(x' - \bar{x}_i')(y' - \bar{y}_i')$	$\Sigma(y' - \bar{y}_i')^2$
1	415·762	59·200	8·609
2	385·657	61·256	9·957
3	435·977	71·931	12·028
4	524·660	120·198	28·150
	1762·06	312·58	58·74

and
$$b = 312 \cdot 58/1762 \cdot 06 = \cdot 17739$$
$$a_1 = (19 \cdot 26 - \cdot 17739 \times 79 \cdot 27)/4 = 1 \cdot 2996$$
$$a_2 = (27 \cdot 06 - \cdot 17739 \times 91 \cdot 59)/4 = 2 \cdot 7032$$
$$a_3 = (32 \cdot 07 - \cdot 17739 \times 97 \cdot 44)/4 = 3 \cdot 6963$$
$$a_4 = (37 \cdot 11 - \cdot 17739 \times 98 \cdot 98)/4 = 4 \cdot 8880$$

The analysis carried out here allows for the possibility of a non-linear dependence of food expenditure on total expenditure, but in actual fact this is not borne out by the results. The difference between successive groups is about 2 persons and about £1.20 on the average for food expenditure with given total expenditure, so that the result is much the same as that obtained by straight multiple regression. Also

$$\Sigma u^2 = 58 \cdot 74 - \cdot 17739 \times 312 \cdot 58$$
$$= 3 \cdot 29$$

and the residual sum of squares is close to the figure of 2·81 obtained previously.

ANSWERS TO EXERCISES

3.1
$$b = 362 \cdot 09/1822 \cdot 16 = \cdot 19871$$
$$a = (115 \cdot 50 - \cdot 19871 \times 367 \cdot 28)/16 = 2 \cdot 6574$$
$$r^2 = \cdot 19871 \times 362 \cdot 09/102 \cdot 19 = \cdot 704$$

With this value of r^2 the simple regression might have been accepted,

43

thus obtaining an erroneous result for $b(b_1)$. This shows the importance of correct specification.

3.2   Addition of ·007 to y', and thus $\Sigma\, y'$, implies

$$\Sigma\, x_1\, y = \cdot067555 + \cdot007\,(\cdot423 - 4\cdot836/9)$$
$$= \cdot067555 - \cdot000800 = \cdot066755$$
$$\Sigma\, x_2\, y = \cdot119163 + \cdot007\,(\cdot242 - 4\cdot073/9)$$
$$= \cdot119163 - \cdot001474 = \cdot117689$$
$$b_1 = 21\cdot63/56\cdot30 = \cdot384$$
$$b_2 = 25\cdot40/56\cdot30 = \cdot451$$

Thus b_1 and b_2 are now nearly equal instead of b_2 being twice as large as b_1.

3.3   In terms of the old variables, $\Sigma\,(x_2 - x_1)^2$, $\Sigma\,(x_2 - x_1)\,(y - x_1)$ and $\Sigma\,(y - x_1)^2$ are required. We have

$$\Sigma\,(x_2 - x_1)^2 = \Sigma\, x_1^2 - 2\Sigma\, x_1\, x_2 + \Sigma\, x_2^2$$
$$= \cdot056736 - 2 \times \cdot099645 + \cdot175998$$
$$= \cdot033444$$
$$\Sigma\,(x_2 - x_1)\,(y - x_1) = \Sigma\, x_1^2 - \Sigma\, x_1\, x_2 - \Sigma\, x_1\, y + \Sigma\, x_2\, y$$
$$= \cdot056736 - \cdot099645 - \cdot067555 + \cdot119163$$
$$= \cdot008699$$
$$\Sigma\,(y - x_1)^2 = \Sigma\, x_1^2 - 2\Sigma\, x_1\, y + \Sigma\, y^2$$
$$= \cdot056736 - 2 \times \cdot067555 + \cdot082017$$
$$= \cdot003643$$

3.4
$$x_i^* = x_i - x_k\,\Sigma\, x_i\, x_k/\Sigma\, x_k^2 \qquad (i = 1, \dots, k-1)$$
$$y^* = y - x_k\,\Sigma\, x_k\, y/\Sigma\, x_k^2$$
$$\Sigma\, x_i^*\, x_j^* = \Sigma\, x_i\, x_j - \Sigma\, x_i\, x_k\,\Sigma\, x_j\, x_k/\Sigma\, x_k^2$$
$$\Sigma\, x_i^*\, y^* = \Sigma\, x_i\, y - \Sigma\, x_i\, x_k\,\Sigma\, x_k\, y/\Sigma\, x_k^2$$

Thus (3.2) with $x_1^*, \dots, x_{k-1}^*$, y^* may be written

$$b_1\,\Sigma\, x_1^2 + \dots + b_{k-1}\,\Sigma\, x_1\, x_{k-1} + \lambda\,\Sigma\, x_1\, x_k = \Sigma\, x_1\, y$$

$$b_1\,\Sigma\, x_1\, x_{k-1} + \dots + b_{k-1}\,\Sigma\, x_{k-1}^2 + \lambda\,\Sigma\, x_{k-1}\, x_k = \Sigma\, x_{k-1}\, y$$

where $\lambda = (\Sigma\, x_k\, y - b_1\,\Sigma\, x_1\, x_k - \dots - b_{k-1}\,\Sigma\, x_{k-1}\, x_k)/\Sigma\, x_k^2$

Hence $b_1\,\Sigma\, x_1\, x_k + \dots + b_{k-1}\,\Sigma\, x_{k-1}\, x_k + \lambda\,\Sigma\, x_k^2 = \Sigma\, x_k\, y.$

If this equation is added to the others, a set of equations (3.2) with k variables is obtained.

3.5 In the multiple regression

$$\Sigma x_1^2 = \cdot033444$$
$$\Sigma x_1 x_2 = 1\cdot401$$
$$\Sigma x_2^2 = 60$$
$$\Sigma x_1 y = \cdot008699$$
$$\Sigma x_2 y = \cdot360$$
$$D = \cdot043839$$
$$b_1 = \cdot017580/D = \cdot401$$
$$b_2 = -\cdot000147459/D = -\cdot00336$$

and the equation is

$$(\log P/L)_c = \text{const.} + \cdot401 \log K/L - \cdot00336\, t$$

The first differences are

x'	y'
·034	·007
·021	·021
·010	−·032
·024	·047
·019	·001
·048	−·001
·022	·010
·003	−·017

	x'	y'
Sum	·181	·036
Mean	·0226	·0045

$$\Sigma x^2 = \cdot005431 - \cdot0040951 = \cdot0013359$$
$$\Sigma xy = \cdot001627 - \cdot0008145 = \cdot0008125$$
$$b = \cdot608$$
$$a = -\cdot00924$$

and the equation may be written as

$$(\log P/L)_c = \text{const.} + \cdot608 \log K/L - \cdot00924\, t$$

4. SIMULTANEOUS EQUATIONS

4.1 Structural equations and reduced form

So far, single regression equations with one dependent variable and a number of independent variables have been considered. An econometric study may contain several relations, with some of the variables occurring in more than one of the equations.

It would be possible to deal with one equation at a time and to estimate the parameters appearing in it by multiple (or simple) regression. There are, however, weighty considerations against a mechanical application of this method. In some cases, the resulting numerical coefficient values are meaningless; in others, they do not provide good estimates of the true parameters. Two kinds of problems thus arise: the problem of identification, and that of estimation.

These difficulties arise only when the dependent variable in one equation reappears as a variable in one or more other equations. In a set of equations in which merely some of the explanatory variables reoccur, such as demand functions for a number of different commodities, no identification or simultaneous estimation problem arises, and the equations may be dealt with one by one.

If, however, some or all of the variables which are to be explained by regression analysis also appear as explanatory variables in the equations, then the distinction between dependent and independent variables which applies to one equation is not valid for the equation system as a whole. Instead, the distinction to be made is that between jointly dependent variables—the influence of which on each other is to be investigated—and predetermined variables, which are considered as exerting an influence on the jointly dependent variables but not as being influenced by them in turn.

Obviously, a lagged variable, referring to a previous period, is invariably treated as predetermined, but current values of some variables may also be so treated. Such variables, which are considered as determined from outside the equation system, are described as " exogenous ", and the variables determined in the system as " endogenous ". The current values of the endogenous variables then constitute the jointly dependent variables; the expression " endogenous " may thus be used in place of " (jointly) dependent ".

Whether a variable is classified as exogenous or endogenous depends on the theoretical scheme or model adopted. Non-economic variables such as climatic conditions will almost invariably be exogenous, but economic variables such as exports and government expenditure may be treated as endogenous in one model and as exogenous in another.

A complete system of simultaneous equations must contain as many equations as there are endogenous variables, but there may be any number of predetermined variables, which may be more or fewer than the endogenous ones. As each endogenous variable must appear at least once, we may formally write each on the left-hand side of one equation with coefficient 1. Furthermore, all variables are taken as deviations from the mean; in practice it is easy to return to the original variables in the end. Thus with h endogenous variables $y_1, ..., y_h$ and k predetermined variables $x_1, ..., x_k$, the system of equations may be written in the general form as follows:

$$\left.\begin{array}{l} y_1 = \beta_{12}\,y_2 + \cdots + \beta_{1h}\,y_h + \gamma_{11}\,x_1 + \cdots + \gamma_{1k}\,x_k + \varepsilon_1 \\ \quad\cdot\quad\cdot\quad\cdot\quad\cdot\quad\cdot\quad\cdot\quad\cdot\quad\cdot\quad\cdot\quad\cdot \\ y_h = \beta_{h1}\,y_1 + \cdots + \beta_{h,\,h-1}\,y_{h-1} + \gamma_{h1}\,x_1 + \cdots + \gamma_{hk}\,x_k + \varepsilon_h \end{array}\right\} \quad (4.1)$$

These equations are called the " structural equations " of the model or set of equations. They show the relationships which are held to exist between the variables on grounds of an established or a new economic theory. The regression coefficients are called the " structural coefficients " in the model, and their number is $h(h-1+k)$.

(4.1) may be written as a set of linear equations for the h variables $y_1, ..., y_h$ expressed as linear functions of the variables $x_1, ..., x_k$. It is implicitly assumed that none of these equations can be expressed as a linear function of the others, in which case one equation would be redundant or the system would be contradictory. Therefore it must be possible to solve the equations for $y_1, ..., y_h$ in such a fashion that each endogenous variable appears as a linear function of the predetermined variables alone, and the set of equations becomes

$$\left.\begin{array}{l} y_1 = \delta_{11}\,x_1 + \cdots + \delta_{1k}\,x_k + \eta_1 \\ \quad\cdot\quad\cdot\quad\cdot\quad\cdot\quad\cdot\quad\cdot \\ y_h = \delta_{h1}\,x_1 + \cdots + \delta_{hk}\,x_k + \eta_h \end{array}\right\} \quad (4.2)$$

where the errors η_i are linear functions of the errors ε_i, and both coefficients δ_{ij} and errors η_i are functions—generally non-linear ones—of the coefficients β_{ij} and γ_{ij}.

(4.2) is called the " reduced form " of the equation system, and the hk coefficients δ_{ij} the " reduced-form coefficients ". By successively regressing $y_1, ..., y_h$ on $x_1, ..., x_k$ together, least-squares estimates d_{ij} of the reduced-form coefficients may be obtained.

What happens if least-square methods are applied to each individual equation of (4.1) instead? It will be seen that the results obtained in this way may not in fact yield estimates of the structural coefficients at all.

47

4.2   Under-identification

For simplicity's sake, the identification problem will be developed for the case $h = 2$, i.e. with two endogenous variables and two equations but any number of predetermined variables. Then (4.1) becomes

$$\left. \begin{array}{l} y_1 = \beta_{12}\, y_2 + \gamma_{11}\, x_1 + \dots + \gamma_{1k}\, x_k + \varepsilon_1 \\ y_2 = \beta_{21}\, y_1 + \gamma_{21}\, x_1 + \dots + \gamma_{2k}\, x_k + \varepsilon_2 \end{array} \right\} \qquad (4.3)$$

Since y_1 and y_2 are jointly dependent, there is no obvious reason for writing y_2 rather than y_1 on the left-hand side of the second equation. By the simple device of moving the term y_2 to the right, the term $\beta_{21}\, y_1$ to the left and dividing by $-\beta_{21}$, the second equation becomes

$$y_1 = y_2/\beta_{21} - \gamma_{21}\, x_1/\beta_{21} - \dots - \gamma_{2k}\, x_k/\beta_{21} - \varepsilon_2/\beta_{21}$$

which is of the same form as the first equation but with different co-efficients. But only one regression of y_1 on $y_2, x_1, \dots, x_k$ can be calculated, and there is no way of telling whether the regression coefficients can be interpreted as $\beta_{12}, \gamma_{11}, \dots, \gamma_{1k}$ or as $1/\beta_{21}, -\gamma_{21}/\beta_{21}, \dots, -\gamma_{2k}/\beta_{21}$.

To make things worse, the equations may be multiplied by the arbitrary factors λ_1 and λ_2, added and divided either by $\lambda_1 - \lambda_2\, \beta_{21}$ or by $\lambda_2 - \lambda_1\, \beta_{12}$. It is easily seen that this procedure results in an un-limited number of additional equations of the same form as the structural ones.

With this state of affairs, we speak of under-identification, and we say that both equations are under-identified. It will be seen that a case may arise when one equation is under-identified but the other is not.

It should be noted that the reduced-form equations are not under-identified. (4.3) can be brought into reduced form as

$$\left. \begin{array}{l} y_1 = \delta_{11}\, x_1 + \dots + \delta_{1k}\, x_k + \eta_1 \\ y_2 = \delta_{21}\, x_1 + \dots + \delta_{2k}\, x_k + \eta_2 \end{array} \right\} \qquad (4.4)$$

These two equations are quite distinct, and the least-squares estimates d_{ik} for the coefficients δ_{ik} have a definite meaning.

If there was only one way in which to combine these equations in order to obtain an equation like the first or second one in (4.3), then estimates for the structural coefficients could be derived from the estimates d_{ik}. But there are many ways of doing this, and the method does not work; it is like trying, after having disentangled a knot, to entangle the strands again as they originally were with nothing to guide one.

It is also clear from counting that estimates of all $2(k+1)$ structural coefficients cannot be derived from the $2k$ reduced-form coefficients.

48

A classical example of under-identification is the case of linear demand and supply relationships operating between quantity sold and price of a commodity, without any predetermined variable entering the analysis ($k = 0$). In general, any apparently observed relationship is then a mixture of demand and supply relations, and neither the demand nor the supply function can be identified. The reduced form is trivial in this case.

The problem was recognized and discussed in the context of demand analysis from its early days on, notably in connection with the result of a positive sloping demand curve for pig iron, obtained by Moore (1914). Notable contributions to the problem were those by E. Working (1927) and Frisch (1933). A systematic approach to identification, together with estimation in simultaneous equations, was made in a series of studies by members of the Cowles Commission; classical papers dealing with the subject are those of Haavelmo (1943) and Koopmans (1949).

Unless further assumptions are made about the disturbances ε_1 and ε_2, there is only one way to escape from the difficulty, and this is to make an *a priori* assumption regarding some of the structural equation coefficients. If a variable does not play an important part in a relation its coefficient may be set equal to zero, and the variable drops out from this equation. Alternatively, some of the coefficients may be equal or be subject to some other restriction.

It is easily seen that the first equation in (4.3) is identified if $\beta_{12} = 0$, as it then coincides with its reduced form and the structural coefficients can be directly estimated. The equation is also identified if any one $\gamma_{1i} = 0$ and $\gamma_{2i} \neq 0$, since no similar equation could then be reproduced as a linear combination of the two equations; any such combination would have a non-zero coefficient for x_i. In this case estimates of the structural coefficients can be derived from estimates of the reduced-form coefficients.

In terms of least-square coefficient estimates, equations (4.4) become

$$\left.\begin{aligned} y_1 &= d_{11}\,x_1 + \ldots + d_{1k}\,x_k + v_1 \\ y_2 &= d_{21}\,x_1 + \ldots + d_{2k}\,x_k + v_2 \end{aligned}\right\} \qquad (4.5)$$

If in (4.3), $\gamma_{1i} = 0$, we look for a linear combination of the equations in (4.5) such that the coefficient of y_1 is 1 and that of x_i is 0. In such a combination $\lambda_1 y_1 + \lambda_2 y_2$ we must have

$$\lambda_1 = 1$$

$$\lambda_1 d_{1i} + \lambda_2 d_{2i} = 0$$

Thus $$\lambda_2 = -d_{1i}/d_{2i}$$

49

The resulting equation then yields estimates b_{12} for β_{12} and c_{1j} for γ_{1j} $(j \neq i)$, for example:

$$b_{12} = d_{1i}/d_{2i}$$

Similarly if, for example, $\gamma_{11} = \gamma_{12}$ but $\gamma_{21} \neq \gamma_{22}$, the first equation in (4.3) is identified. Estimates for its coefficients are then obtained from (4.5) by multiplying the equations by 1 and λ respectively, such that

$$d_{11} + \lambda d_{21} = d_{12} + \lambda d_{22}$$

Thus
$$\lambda = (d_{11} - d_{12})/(d_{22} - d_{21})$$

In the resulting equation, the coefficients of x_1 and x_2 will be the same.

If a similar parameter restriction applies to the second equation as well, then both equations are identified and we speak of an identified equation system. With $k \geqslant 2$, for example, $\gamma_{1k} = 0$ and $\gamma_{21} = 0$ will give an identified system (provided that $\gamma_{11} \neq 0$, $\gamma_{2k} \neq 0$). If there are no further parameter restrictions, there are as many structural as reduced-form parameters; and all the former can be derived from the latter. This method of estimating the structural coefficients is known as indirect least squares, or the reduced-form method.

Exercise 4.1 In the model

$$y_1 = \beta_{12} y_2 + \gamma_{11} x_1 + \varepsilon_1$$
$$y_2 = \beta_{21} y_1 + \gamma_{22} x_2 + \varepsilon_2$$

derive explicit formulae for b_{12}, b_{21}, c_{11} and c_{22} in terms of d_{11}, d_{12}, d_{21} and d_{22}.

In (4.3), a case which is worth noting is that of $\beta_{12} = 0$ whilst $\beta_{21} \neq 0$ and all $\gamma_{ij} \neq 0$. In this case, the first equation is identified but the second one is not. In the second equation, y_1 can be considered as one of the independent variables together with $x_1, ..., x_k$. y_1 does not depend on y_2, but according to the first equation a relationship exists between $y_1, x_1, ..., x_k$ which are the explanatory variables of the second equation. The second equation is under-identified since we have multicollinearity, and the individual coefficients cannot be estimated. This shows the link between multicollinearity and under-identification: it is the existence of too many relationships between the same variables which makes estimation impossible.

The concepts of identification and under-identification may be readily generalized to systems of more than two equations. According to the structure of the model, any equation may be identified or not. Under the usual assumptions, identification is achieved only by omission of variables or other parameter restrictions.

It might be thought at first that the omission of a different variable from each equation sufficed to make the whole system identified, but this is not true. With h equations, there are $h-1$ equations besides the one under consideration, and by linear combination an equation with $h-2$ zero coefficients or other parameter restrictions can be constructed. If the first equation has fewer than $h-1$ zero coefficients (or restrictions), an equation of similar form can be obtained by linear combination, and the equation is not identified.

A necessary condition for identification is therefore the existence of at least $h-1$ parameter restrictions in the equation. Since the coefficient of one dependent variable is set at unity, this implies the appearance of no more than k different parameters for estimation in each equation.

The simplest case is that in which all restrictions imply the requisite number of zero coefficients. In this case the additional condition which helps to make up a set of necessary and sufficient conditions is easily formulated. Take the variables excluded from the equation studied, and write down their coefficients in the remaining equations. From these coefficients it must be possible to form at least one non-vanishing determinant of $h-1$ rows and columns. If this condition is not satisfied, an equation with zero coefficients for the variables under consideration can be constructed and identification falls to the ground.

Exercise 4.2 Show that in the following system:

$$y_1 = \beta_{12} y_2 + \beta_{13} y_3 + \gamma_{11} x_1$$
$$y_2 = \beta_{23} y_3 \qquad\qquad + \gamma_{21} x_1 + \gamma_{22} x_2$$
$$y_3 = \beta_{31} y_1 \qquad\qquad + \gamma_{31} x_1 + \gamma_{32} x_2$$
$$y_4 = \beta_{41} y_1 + \beta_{42} y_2 \qquad\qquad\qquad + \gamma_{43} x_3$$

only the last equation is identified.

In the general case of parameter restrictions there is no such simple counting rule, and greater care is needed to ascertain identifiability from the structural equations.

It is also possible to deduce the identification properties from the reduced form. If an equation is identified, the structural parameters may be estimated with the help of the reduced form; if it is underidentified this is impossible. A proof of the equivalence of the two identifiability criteria has been given by Koopmans and Hood (1953).

With h endogenous and k predetermined variables, a system of h equations, neither of which contains more than k parameters, is usually fully identified. In the model of Exercise 4.2, which forms an apparent exception, the variable x_3 does not enter the reduced-form equations for y_1, y_2 and y_3, hence identification is not achieved.

4.3 Estimation in identified equation systems

From now on, all equations in the set under consideration will be assumed to be identified. Unless this assumption is satisfied, proper estimation of structural equations is not possible, though the reduced-form equations may still be estimated.

The parameters of the identified structural equations may be estimated directly by single-equation least squares, and estimates for the reduced-form coefficients can then be deduced. Alternatively, the reduced-form coefficients may be estimated first by indirect least squares, i.e. by applying least squares to the reduced form; and in some circumstances, estimates of the structural coefficients can be readily derived. The two sets of estimates will generally differ from each other, as can be seen from the example of the very simple model:

$$y_1 = \gamma x + \varepsilon_1$$
$$y_2 = \beta y_1 + \varepsilon_2$$

The first equation coincides with its reduced form, but the reduced form of the second equation is

$$y_2 = \beta\gamma x + (\beta\varepsilon_1 + \varepsilon_2)$$

Single-equation estimation yields

$$b(\text{SE}) = \Sigma\, y_1\, y_2 / \Sigma\, y_1^2$$
$$c(\text{SE}) = \Sigma\, x\, y_1 / \Sigma\, x^2$$

Thus, if d is the estimate for $\delta = \beta\gamma$,

$$. \ d(\text{SE}) = \Sigma\, x\, y_1\, \Sigma\, y_1\, y_2 / \Sigma\, x^2\, \Sigma\, y_1^2$$

Indirect least squares lead to

$$c(\text{IL}) = \Sigma\, x\, y_1 / \Sigma\, x^2 = c(\text{SE})$$

but

$$d(\text{IL}) = \Sigma\, x\, y_2 / \Sigma\, x^2 \neq d(\text{SE})$$
$$b(\text{IL}) = d(\text{IL})/c(\text{IL})$$
$$= \Sigma\, x\, y_2 / \Sigma\, x\, y_1 \neq b(\text{SE})$$

If two different estimation methods are applicable and lead to different results, the question is: which, if any, is to be preferred? It will be shown that single-equation estimation generally leads to results which are biased and not consistent and for this reason is frequently rejected.

Consider the identified version of (4.3)

$$\begin{aligned}
y_1 &= \beta_{12} y_2 + \gamma_{11} x_1 + \gamma_{12} x_2 + \cdots + \gamma_{1,\, k-1} x_{k-1} && + \varepsilon_1 \\
y_2 &= \beta_{21} y_1 && + \gamma_{22} x_2 + \cdots + \gamma_{2,\, k-1} x_{k-1} + \gamma_{2,\, k} x_k + \varepsilon_2
\end{aligned}\Biggr\}$$

$$(4.6)$$

with its reduced form (4.4).

Applying least squares to the second structural equation and writing

$$
D = \begin{vmatrix}
\Sigma y_1^2 & \Sigma x_2 y_1 & \dots & \Sigma x_k y_1 \\
\Sigma x_2 y_1 & \Sigma x_2^2 & \dots & \Sigma x_2 x_k \\
\cdot & \cdot & \cdot & \cdot \\
\Sigma x_k y_1 & \Sigma x_2 x_k & \dots & \Sigma x_k^2
\end{vmatrix}
$$

and $A_{11}, A_{12}, \dots, A_{1k}$ for the co-factors of $\Sigma y_1^2, \Sigma x_2 y_1, \dots, \Sigma x_k y_1$ respectively, we have, for example:

$$
b_{21} = (A_{11} \Sigma y_1 y_2 + A_{12} \Sigma x_2 y_2 + \dots + A_{1k} \Sigma x_k y_2)/D
$$

and according to (3.5)

$$
b_{21} = \beta_{21} + (A_{11} \Sigma \varepsilon_2 y_1 + A_{12} \Sigma \varepsilon_2 x_2 + \dots + A_{1k} \Sigma \varepsilon_2 x_k)/D
$$

But $\qquad\qquad y_1 = \delta_{11} x_1 + \dots + \delta_{1k} x_k + \eta_1$

with $\qquad\qquad \eta_1 = (\varepsilon_1 + \beta_{12} \varepsilon_2)/(1 - \beta_{12} \beta_{21})$

Thus we can write, with constants $C_1, \dots, C_k$ and C which also depend on y_1 but need not be written down explicitly,

$$
b_{21} = \beta_{21} + C_1 \Sigma \varepsilon_2 x_1 + \dots + C_k \Sigma \varepsilon_2 x_k
$$
$$
+ C (\Sigma \varepsilon_1 \varepsilon_2 + \beta_{12} \Sigma \varepsilon_2^2)/(1 - \beta_{12} \beta_{21})
$$

and clearly $\qquad\qquad E(b_{21}) \neq \beta_{21}$

Thus b_{21} is biased, and the difference does not tend to disappear with increasing length of the observation series. Thus b_{21} is not a consistent estimator; and the same applies to the estimators for the other coefficients.

The indirect least-squares method gives unbiased and consistent estimates for the reduced-form coefficients, though with the usual error specification they are generally not fully efficient. The structural co-efficient estimates to which the method leads are generally biased but are invariably consistent. The method is therefore usually preferred to single-equation estimation.

There is, however, one case in which the position is different: this is the case of a so-called recursive system. With two equations, the case arises if in (4.3) $\beta_{12} = 0$ (or $\beta_{21} = 0$) and $E(\varepsilon_1 \varepsilon_2) = 0$. In these circumstances, there is only a one-way relationship and no real interdependence between the two variables y_1 and y_2.

The assumption about the independence of the errors ε_1 and ε_2 at the same time guarantees the identification of both equations without the exclusion of a further variable besides y_2 from the first equation. Indeed, with this assumption, equation system (4.3) is also identified provided only one of the coefficients $\gamma_{ij} = 0$; for the property of independent disturbance terms does not hold for linear combinations of the structural equations. But the assumption appears more realistic when $\beta_{12} = 0$ as a causal chain from y_1 to y_2 can then be said to exist.

The equation system can be written as

$$
\left.\begin{aligned}
y_1 &= \phantom{\beta_{21}y_1+} \gamma_{11}x_1+\dots+\gamma_{1k}x_k+\varepsilon_1 \\
y_2 &= \beta_{21}y_1+\gamma_{21}x_1+\dots+\gamma_{2k}x_k+\varepsilon_2
\end{aligned}\right\}
\tag{4.7}
$$

As with (4.6) we obtain an expression

$$
b_{21} = \beta_{21}+(A_{10}\Sigma\,\varepsilon_2 y_1+A_{11}\Sigma\,\varepsilon_2 x_1+\dots+A_{1k}\Sigma\,\varepsilon_2 x_k)/D
$$

and using the first equation in (4.7):

$$
b_{21} = \beta_{21}+C_1\Sigma\,\varepsilon_2 x_1+\dots+C_k\Sigma\,\varepsilon_2 x_k+C\Sigma\,\varepsilon_1\varepsilon_2
$$

Thus $E(b_{21}) = \beta_{21}$.

b_{21} is an unbiased estimator of β_{21} and it is not difficult to see that it is consistent. The same obviously applies to the estimates for the other coefficients.

In a recursive model, then, both single-equation and reduced-form methods lead to consistent estimates, whilst the former gives unbiased estimates for the structural parameters, the latter for the reduced-form parameters. The single-equation estimators are optimal with the usual error specification; moreover, they can be shown to be maximum-likelihood estimates if the errors are normally distributed. These properties were first pointed out by Bentzel and Wold (1946).

In the general two-equation model, the likelihood function for the errors ε_1, ε_2 is, assuming their independence,

$$
L = (2\pi)^{-n}\,(\sigma_1\,\sigma_2)^{-n}\exp\left(-\Sigma\,\varepsilon_1^2/2\sigma_1^2-\Sigma\,\varepsilon_2^2/2\sigma_2^2\right)
$$

but in the likelihood function for the observations y_1, y_2 this expression is multiplied by the Jacobian determinant

$$
\Delta =
\begin{vmatrix}
\dfrac{\partial\varepsilon_1}{\partial y_1} & \dfrac{\partial\varepsilon_1}{\partial y_2} \\[2ex]
\dfrac{\partial\varepsilon_2}{\partial y_1} & \dfrac{\partial\varepsilon_2}{\partial y_2}
\end{vmatrix}
=
\begin{vmatrix}
1 & -\beta_{12} \\[1ex]
-\beta_{21} & 1
\end{vmatrix}
$$

$$
= 1-\beta_{12}\beta_{21}
$$

and the presence of this term leads to complicated non-linear expressions.

With the recursive model, however,

$$
\Delta = 1
$$

$$
-\log L = n\log 2\pi+n(\log\sigma_1+\log\sigma_2)+\Sigma\,\varepsilon_1^2/2\sigma_1^2+\Sigma\,\varepsilon_2^2/2\sigma_2^2
$$

and minimization of this expression leads to the usual least-square conditions for the structural equations as well as the (biased) maximum-likelihood estimates for the error variances

$$s_1^2 = \Sigma\, u_1^2/n$$
$$s_2^2 = \Sigma\, u_2^2/n$$

$\Sigma\, u_1^2$, $\Sigma\, u_2^2$ being the residual sums of squares.

Example 4.1 With a demand and supply relationship between price p and quantity q, neither equation is identified. If, however, the price in the supply equation carries a time-lag such that

$$q = \alpha_1 + \gamma p_{-1} + \varepsilon_1'$$
$$p = \alpha_2 + \beta q + \varepsilon_2'$$

then writing x' for p_{-1}, y_1' for q, and y_2' for p, we obtain the model

$$y_1 = \gamma x + \varepsilon_1$$

$$y_2 = \beta y_1 + \varepsilon_2$$

which is recursive and identified. Although this may seem paradoxical at first, two equations can be estimated from virtually two series of observations.

An artificial series of 15 data is obtained from the relations

$$y_1' = 3x' + \varepsilon_1'$$

$$y_2' = 16 - \cdot 2 y_1' + \varepsilon_2'$$

where ε_1 assumes the values -5, 0, $+5$, and ε_2 the values -2, 0, $+2$ with probability $\frac{1}{3}$ each, and their values are obtained by random numbers. Also $x' = 15$ is specified for the initial value, and y_2' provides the further values of x':

ε_1'	ε_2'	x'	y_1'	y_2'
-5	-2	15·0	40·0	6·0
-5	-2	6·0	13·0	11·4
$+5$	-2	11·4	39·2	6·2
0	0	6·2	18·6	12·3
$+5$	$+2$	12·3	41·9	9·6
-5	0	9·6	23·8	11·2
-5	-2	11·2	28·6	8·3
-5	$+2$	8·3	19·9	14·0
$+5$	0	14·0	47·0	6·6
$+5$	0	6·6	24·8	11·0
$+5$	-2	11·0	38·0	6·4
$+5$	0	6·4	24·2	11·2
$+5$	-2	11·2	38·6	6·3
0	$+2$	6·3	18·9	14·2
-5	0	14·2	37·6	8·5
Sum $+5$	-6	149·7	454·1	143·2

$$\Sigma\, x^2 = 1\,635\cdot47 - 1\,494\cdot01 = 141\cdot46$$

$$\Sigma\, xy_1 = 4\,949\cdot41 - 4\,531\cdot92 = 417\cdot49$$

$$\Sigma\, y_1^2 = 15\,302\cdot23 - 13\,747\cdot12 = 1\,555\cdot11$$

$$\Sigma\, y_1\, y_2 = 3\,973\cdot20 - 4\,335\cdot14 = -361\cdot94$$

Thus single-equation estimation for $\gamma = 3$ and $\beta = -\cdot2$ yields

$$c = 417\cdot49/141\cdot46 = 2\cdot951$$

$$b = -361\cdot94/1\,555\cdot11 = -\cdot233$$

and thus gives quite good results.

Exercise 4.3 Obtain an alternative estimate for β by the reduced-form method.

In the general case of h equations, a recursive system may, by suitable numbering of the endogenous variables, be written as follows

$$\left.\begin{aligned}
y_1 &= & \gamma_{11}\, x_1 + \ldots + \gamma_{1k}\, x_k + \varepsilon_1 \\
y_2 &= \beta_{21}\, y_1 & +\gamma_{21}\, x_1 + \ldots + \gamma_{2k}\, x_k + \varepsilon_2 \\
&\;\;\cdot \qquad\cdot \qquad\qquad \cdot \qquad\qquad\qquad \cdot \\
y_h &= \beta_{h1}\, y_1 + \ldots + \beta_{h,\,h-1}\, y_{h-1} + \gamma_{h1}\, x_1 + \ldots + \gamma_{hk}\, x_k + \varepsilon_h
\end{aligned}\right\} \quad (4.8)$$

where the coefficient scheme of the y_i is triangular, with zeros above and to the right of the main diagonal, and moreover

$$E(\varepsilon_i \varepsilon_j) = 0 \text{ for all } j \neq i$$

In this equation system, which is always fully identified, single-equation estimation leads to best unbiased, and of course consistent, linear estimates of the coefficients. With normally distributed disturbances in the structural equations, the results are also equivalent to maximum-likelihood estimates.

4.4 Over-identified equations

We return once more to the two-equation model (4.3) as a starting-point. The omission of one variable from an equation has been shown to make that equation identified. The question now arises what happens if more than one variable is omitted from one equation whilst being retained in the other, or more generally, if more than one restriction is imposed on the parameters of one equation.

Consider the model

$$\left.\begin{aligned}
y_1 &= \beta_{12}\, y_2 + \gamma_{11}\, x_1 + \ldots + \gamma_{1,\,k-1}\, x_{k-1} + \varepsilon_1 \\
y_2 &= \beta_{21}\, y_1 + \gamma_{23}\, x_3 + \ldots + \gamma_{2k}\, x_k + \varepsilon_2
\end{aligned}\right\} \quad (4.9)$$

If the reduced-form coefficients are estimated, equations of the form (4.5) are again obtained, and it is easy to obtain a linear combination with a zero coefficient for x_k from which estimates for the coefficients in the first structural equation are derived. But it will usually be impossible to construct an equation with zero coefficients for both x_1 and x_2, and the reduced-form method breaks down.

It would of course be possible to ignore the condition

$$\lambda d_{12} + d_{22} = 0$$

and merely specify λ so that

$$\lambda d_{11} + d_{21} = 0$$

thus obtaining structural coefficient estimates based on the ratio d_{12}/d_{11}. But alternatively, the ratio d_{22}/d_{21} may be utilized, and the two sets of estimates will be conflicting. This is clearly unsatisfactory.

We say that the equation is over-identified. This does not imply that the structural coefficients cannot be estimated but merely that methods other than the reduced-form method, which ignores some of the parameter restrictions, should be used.

Over-identification does not seriously matter with a recursive system since the single-equation approach is permissible and indeed recommended here, and with this method no estimation difficulties arise.

With a non-recursive system the solution is not so obvious, as various simultaneous equation estimation methods are available. The simplest method, developed by Basmann (1957) and Theil (1961), is that of two-stage least squares. Its basic idea consists in replacing, in any one over-identified equation, the endogenous variables appearing on the right-hand side by their theoretical values derived from the reduced-form equations. Ordinary least squares may then be applied to the new set of variables. For example, in the second equation of the system (4.9), the variable y_1 is replaced by y_{1c}, where

$$y_{1c} = d_{11}x_1 + \dots + d_{1k}x_k = y_1 - v_1$$

The effect of this procedure is to eliminate, as far as possible, the error term η_1 and with it the source of asymptotic bias. The resulting estimates are consistent.

In practice it is not necessary to compute explicitly the theoretical values of the endogenous variables, since the sums of squares and cross products containing them may be obtained directly with the help of the reduced-form equations. In the general case, with h jointly dependent and k predetermined variables, it follows from least-squares properties that

$$\Sigma y_{ic}x_j = \Sigma y_i x_j$$

$$\Sigma y_{ic}y_j = d_{i1}\Sigma x_1 y_j + \dots + d_{ik}\Sigma x_k y_j$$

$$= d_{j1}\Sigma x_1 y_i + \dots + d_{jk}\Sigma x_k y_i = \Sigma y_{jc}y_i$$

If the two-stage least-squares method is applied to a just-identified equation, the result is the same as that of indirect least squares. For example, if we substitute for y_2 in the first equation of (4.9) the regression

$$y_{2c} = d_{21} x_1 + \dots + d_{2k} x_k$$

the equation becomes

$$y_1 = \gamma_{11} x_1 + \dots + \gamma_{1, k-1} x_{k-1} + \beta_{12} y_{2c} + \varepsilon_1$$

$$= (\beta_{12} d_{21} + \gamma_{11}) x_1 + \dots + (\beta_{12} d_{2, k-1} + \gamma_{2, k-1}) x_{k-1}$$

$$+ \beta_{12} d_{2k} x_k + \varepsilon_1$$

As **both** formulations involve multiple regression on k variables, estimation is equivalent, and the coefficient estimates in the second expression are equal to the reduced-form coefficients; thus

$$d_{1i} = b_{12} d_{2i} + c_{1i} \qquad (i = 1, \dots, k-1)$$

$$d_{1k} = b_{12} d_{2k}$$

from which it follows that

$$b_{12} = d_{1k}/d_{2k}$$

$$c_{1i} = d_{1i} - d_{2i} d_{1k}/d_{2k} \qquad (i = 1, \dots, k-1)$$

But indirect least squares gives

$$y_1 = (d_{1k}/d_{2k}) y_2 + (d_{11} - d_{21} d_{1k}/d_{2k}) x_1 +$$

$$+ \dots + (d_{1, k-1} - d_{2, k-1} d_{1k}/d_{2k}) x_{k-1} + u_1$$

Thus the two methods are equivalent in this case.

Another commonly encountered method, which is actually older than two-stage least squares, is the limited-information maximum-likelihood method, briefly referred to as " limited-information method ". It is based on the maximum-likelihood principle, assuming the errors to be normally distributed. The full maximum-likelihood method, which is also sometimes used, follows the maximizing conditions strictly but may lead to complicated non-linear expressions, even with the assumption of independent disturbances in the various structural equations.

The limited-information method ignores, in the estimation of one equation, the parameter restriction affecting other equations, and this makes the system easier to handle. A classical exposition of the method and the computations involved was given by Girshick and Haavelmo (1947); the theory was developed, in particular, by Anderson and Rubin (1949). It has been shown that the method minimizes the ratio of certain variances, and for this reason it is also sometimes referred to as " least variance ratio method ". The variances in question refer to the residuals after regression on the predetermined variables in the equation concerned and on all predetermined variables in the system respectively; and the estimators minimize the improvement in fit which addition of the excluded variables would bring. The calculations involved, as also the full maximum likelihood calculations in a single case, will be illustrated by the example which follows. For just-identified equations, the limited-information estimates, like the two-stage least-squares estimates, are identical with the indirect least-squares estimates.

Example 4.2　The model shown here represents a first version of a simple experimental forecasting model for Ireland. The variables are:

$y_1' = Y$　　gross national product,
$y_2' = C$　　personal expenditure,
$x_1' = D$　　final demand other than personal expenditure,
$x_2' = Y_{-1}$　gross national product lagged one year.

The model consists of a production decision function and a consumption function, described respectively by the equations

$$Y = \alpha_1 + \beta_{12}(C + D) + \varepsilon_1'$$
$$C = \alpha_2 + \beta_{21} Y + \gamma_{22} Y_{-1} + \varepsilon_2'$$

and the first equation implies the existence of an import decision function since, with imports M,

$$M = C + D - Y$$

The structural equations can be written as

$$y_1 = \beta_{12}(y_2 + x_1) + \varepsilon_1$$
$$y_2 = \beta_{21}y_1 + \gamma_{22}x_2 + \varepsilon_2$$

The second equation is exactly identified. The first equation is over-identified owing to the restriction $\gamma_{11} = \beta_{12}$; if the restriction was dropped the equation would also be just identified.

The data, supplied by the Irish C.S.O. (1962), refer to the nine year-to-year first differences 1953/4 to 1961/2 in current prices (in £ mill.) and are as follows:

$D = x_1'$	$Y_{-1} = x_2'$	$Y = y_1'$	$C = y_2'$
$-6\cdot8$	$46\cdot7$	$3\cdot1$	$7\cdot4$
$22\cdot4$	$3\cdot1$	$22\cdot8$	$30\cdot4$
$-17\cdot3$	$22\cdot8$	$7\cdot8$	$1\cdot3$
$12\cdot0$	$7\cdot8$	$21\cdot4$	$8\cdot7$
$5\cdot9$	$21\cdot4$	$17\cdot8$	$25\cdot8$
$44\cdot7$	$17\cdot8$	$37\cdot2$	$8\cdot6$
$23\cdot1$	$37\cdot2$	$35\cdot7$	$30\cdot0$
$51\cdot2$	$35\cdot7$	$46\cdot6$	$31\cdot4$
$32\cdot3$	$46\cdot6$	$56\cdot0$	$39\cdot1$
Sum $167\cdot5$	$239\cdot1$	$248\cdot4$	$182\cdot7$

Routine computations give:

$$\Sigma x_1^2 = 4105\cdot17 \qquad \Sigma x_1 y_2 = 1412\cdot55$$
$$\Sigma x_1 x_2 = 115\cdot38 \qquad \Sigma x_2 y_2 = 447\cdot83$$
$$\Sigma x_2^2 = 2023\cdot78 \qquad \Sigma y_1^2 = 2475\cdot14$$
$$\Sigma x_1 y_1 = 2775\cdot75 \qquad \Sigma y_1 y_2 = 1372\cdot86$$
$$\Sigma x_2 y_1 = 605\cdot39 \qquad \Sigma y_2^2 = 1501\cdot86$$

It is also useful to compute the expressions

$$\Sigma(y_2 + x_1)y_1 = \Sigma y_1 y_2 + \Sigma x_1 y_1 = 4148\cdot61$$
$$\Sigma(y_2 + x_1)^2 = \Sigma y_2^2 + 2\Sigma x_1 y_2 + \Sigma x_1^2 = 8432\cdot13$$

The various estimation methods may then be employed, to be considered successively.

(a) *Single-equation least squares*

$$b_{12}(\text{SE}) = \Sigma(y_2 + x_1)y_1/\Sigma(y_2 + x_1)^2 = \cdot4920$$
$$b_{21}(\text{SE}) = (\Sigma x_2^2 \Sigma y_1 y_2 - \Sigma x_2 y_1 \Sigma x_2 y_2)/[\Sigma y_1^2 \Sigma x_2^2 - (\Sigma x_2 y_1)^2]$$
$$= 2\,507\,255/4\,642\,642 = \cdot5400$$
$$c_{22}(\text{SE}) = (\Sigma y_1^2 \Sigma x_2 y_2 - \Sigma x_2 y_1 \Sigma y_1 y_2)/[\Sigma y_1^2 \Sigma x_2^2 - (\Sigma x_2 y_1)^2]$$
$$= 277\,326/4\,642\,642 = \cdot0597$$

Although the method does not yield consistent estimators, nevertheless the estimates convey an idea regarding the magnitude of the coefficients and are therefore useful. At the same time the coefficients of determination may be obtained for the structural equations

$$R_1^2 = b_{12}(\text{SE}) \Sigma(y_2+x_1)y_1/\Sigma y_1^2$$
$$= 2041 \cdot 12/2475 \cdot 14 = \cdot 825$$
$$R_2^2 = [b_{21}(\text{SE}) \Sigma y_1 y_2 + c_{22}(\text{SE}) \Sigma x_2 y_2]/\Sigma y_2^2$$
$$= 768 \cdot 08/1501 \cdot 86 = \cdot 511$$

The consumption function does not give a good fit to the data; for this and other reasons, the model was modified at this stage before going any further. It will, however, serve for the present purpose of illustrating econometric estimation methods.

In the reduced form

$$y_1 = d_{11}x_1 + d_{12}x_2 + v_1$$
$$y_2 = d_{21}x_1 + d_{22}x_2 + v_2$$

it is clearly seen that

$$d_{11} = b_{12}/(1 - b_{12}b_{21})$$
$$d_{12} = b_{12}c_{22}/(1 - b_{12}b_{21})$$
$$d_{21} = b_{12}b_{21}/(1 - b_{12}b_{21})$$
$$d_{22} = c_{22}/(1 - b_{12}b_{21})$$

and we may therefore, if desired, arrive at estimates of the reduced form coefficients as follows:

$$d_{11}(\text{SE}) = \cdot 4920/\cdot 73432 = \cdot 6700$$
$$d_{12}(\text{SE}) = \cdot 02937/\cdot 73432 = \cdot 0400$$
$$d_{21}(\text{SE}) = \cdot 26568/\cdot 73432 = \cdot 3618$$
$$d_{22}(\text{SE}) = \cdot 0597/\cdot 73432 = \cdot 0813$$

(b) *Indirect least squares*

$$d_{11}(\text{IL}) = (\Sigma x_2^2 \Sigma x_1 y_1 - \Sigma x_1 x_2 \Sigma x_2 y_1)/[\Sigma x_1^2 \Sigma x_2^2 - (\Sigma x_1 x_2)^2]$$
$$= 5547657/8294648 = \cdot 6688$$
$$d_{12}(\text{IL}) = (\Sigma x_1^2 \Sigma x_2 y_1 - \Sigma x_1 x_2 \Sigma x_1 y_1)/[\Sigma x_1^2 \Sigma x_2^2 - (\Sigma x_1 x_2)^2]$$
$$= 2164963/8294648 = \cdot 2610$$
$$d_{21}(\text{IL}) = (\Sigma x_2^2 \Sigma x_1 y_2 - \Sigma x_1 x_2 \Sigma x_2 y_2)/[\Sigma x_1^2 \Sigma x_2^2 - (\Sigma x_1 x_2)^2]$$
$$= 2807020/8294648 = \cdot 3384$$
$$d_{22}(\text{IL}) = (\Sigma x_1^2 \Sigma x_2 y_2 - \Sigma x_1 x_2 \Sigma x_1 y_2)/[\Sigma x_1^2 \Sigma x_2^2 - (\Sigma x_1 x_2)^2]$$
$$= 1675438/8294648 = \cdot 2020$$

Furthermore

$$R_3^2 = [d_{11}(IL)\Sigma x_1 y_1 + d_{12}(IL)\Sigma x_2 y_1]/\Sigma y_1^2$$
$$= 2014\cdot43/2475\cdot14 = \cdot814$$
$$R_4^2 = [d_{21}(IL)\Sigma x_1 y_2 + d_{22}(IL)\Sigma x_2 y_2]/\Sigma y_2^2$$
$$= 568\cdot47/1501\cdot86 = \cdot379$$

Again the fit is good for gross national product but poor for consumption.

The first equation is over-identified, and its structural coefficient cannot be estimated by indirect least squares. For the second equation, which is exactly identified, we use the relations

$$b_{21} = d_{21}/d_{11}$$
$$c_{22} = (d_{11}d_{22} - d_{12}d_{21})/d_{11}$$

Hence
$$b_{21}(IL) = \cdot3384/\cdot6688 = \cdot5060$$
$$c_{22}(IL) = \cdot046\,78/\cdot6688 = \cdot0699$$

(c) *Two-stage least squares*

When using this method, the first equation becomes for practical purposes

$$y_1 = \beta_{12}(y_{2c} + x_1) + \varepsilon_1$$

We therefore require the expressions

$$\Sigma(y_{2c} + x_1)^2 = \Sigma y_{2c}^2 + 2\Sigma x_1 y_{2c} + \Sigma x_1^2$$

and
$$\Sigma(y_{2c} + x_1)y_1 = \Sigma y_1 y_{2c} + \Sigma x_1 y_1$$

Now
$$\Sigma x_1 y_{2c} = \Sigma x_1 y_2 = 1412\cdot55$$

and in deriving R_4^2 we have already established that

$$\Sigma y_{2c}^2 = 568\cdot47$$

hence
$$\Sigma(y_{2c} + x_1)^2 = 568\cdot47 + 2825\cdot10 + 4105\cdot17 = 7498\cdot74$$

Furthermore

$$\Sigma y_1 y_{2c} = d_{11}(IL)\Sigma x_1 y_2 + d_{12}(IL)\Sigma x_2 y_2$$
$$= d_{21}(IL)\Sigma x_1 y_1 + d_{22}(IL)\Sigma x_1 y_2$$

the double calculation acting as a check; the result is

$$\Sigma y_1 y_{2c} = 1061\cdot60$$
$$\Sigma(y_{2c} + x_1)y_1 = 1061\cdot60 + 2775\cdot75 = 3837\cdot35$$

By simple least squares, therefore

$$b_{12}(\text{TS}) = \Sigma(y_{2c}+x_1)y_1/\Sigma(y_{2c}+x_1)^2$$
$$= \cdot 5117$$

Exercise 4.4 Verify that for the second equation

$$b_{21}(\text{TS}) = b_{21}(\text{IL}) = \cdot 5060$$
$$c_{22}(\text{TS}) = c_{22}(\text{IL}) = \cdot 0699$$

The two-stage estimates were based on the reduced-form coefficients but may now be used to revise them in order to make them conform with the parameter restriction $c_{11} = b_{12}$. Proceeding as in the case of single-equation estimation, we obtain the results

$$d_{11}(\text{TS}) = \cdot 5117/\cdot 74108 \;\; = \cdot 6905$$
$$d_{12}(\text{TS}) = \cdot 03577/\cdot 74108 = \cdot 0483$$
$$d_{21}(\text{TS}) = \cdot 25892/\cdot 74108 = \cdot 3494$$
$$d_{22}(\text{TS}) = \cdot 0699/\cdot 74108 \;\; = \cdot 0943$$

(d) *Limited-information maximum likelihood*

This method makes no distinction between variables appearing on the left-hand and right-hand sides of the structural equations; the equation system may therefore be written as

$$-y_1 + \beta_{12}(y_2+x_1) + \varepsilon_1 = 0$$
$$\beta_{21}y_1 - y_2 + \gamma_{22}x_2 + \varepsilon_2 = 0$$

As in the case of two-stage least squares, we use the theoretical values of the endogenous variables, based on the reduced form with all predetermined variables. For the first equation, we know that

$$\Sigma y_{1c}^2 = 2014\cdot 43$$
$$\Sigma y_{1c}(y_{2c}+x_1) = 3837\cdot 35$$
$$\Sigma(y_{2c}+x_1)^2 = 7498\cdot 74$$

These expressions are utilized in the derivation of the residual sums

$$\Sigma y_1^2 - \Sigma y_{1c}^2 = 460\cdot 71$$
$$\Sigma y_1(y_2+x_1) - \Sigma y_{1c}(y_{2c}+x_1) = 311\cdot 26$$
$$\Sigma(y_2+x_1)^2 - \Sigma(y_{2c}+x_1)^2 = 933\cdot 39$$

We also require the residual sums after regression on the predetermined variables appearing by themselves in the first equation. In this case, x_1 does not count as it is combined with y_2, and x_2 does not appear in the equation; hence the residual sums coincide with the original sums

$$\Sigma y_1^2 = 2475 \cdot 14$$
$$\Sigma y_1(y_2 + x_1) = 4148 \cdot 61$$
$$\Sigma(y_2 + x_1)^2 = 8432 \cdot 13$$

For the estimation of $b_{12}(\text{LI})$ the method makes use of the equations, in which the coefficients of y_1 and y_2 in the first structural equation appear.

$$(2475 \cdot 14 - 460 \cdot 71\lambda)(-1) + (4148 \cdot 61 - 311 \cdot 26\lambda)b_{12} = 0$$
$$(4148 \cdot 61 - 311 \cdot 26\lambda)(-1) + (8432 \cdot 13 - 933 \cdot 39\lambda)b_{12} = 0$$

which can be solved if and only if

$$\begin{vmatrix} 2475 \cdot 14 - 460 \cdot 71\lambda & 4148 \cdot 61 - 311 \cdot 26 \\ 4148 \cdot 61 - 311 \cdot 26\lambda & 8432 \cdot 13 - 933 \cdot 39 \end{vmatrix} = 0$$

or
$$333139\lambda^2 - 3612445\lambda + 3659737 = 0$$
$$\lambda^2 - 10 \cdot 844\lambda + 10 \cdot 986 = 0$$

The relevant solution is the smallest value of λ that satisfies the equation; here

$$\lambda = (10 \cdot 844 - \sqrt{73 \cdot 6483})/2 = 1 \cdot 131$$

Substituting this value of λ into, say, the first of the two equations for b_{12}, we find that

$$-1954 \cdot 08 + 3796 \cdot 57 b_{12}(\text{LI}) = 0$$
$$b_{12}(\text{LI}) = \cdot 5147$$

Although it is not necessary to apply the method to the second equation, it may be instructive to do so. In the first place, we obtain the same residual sums as before:

$$\Sigma y_1^2 - \Sigma y_{1c}^2 = 460 \cdot 71$$
$$\Sigma y_1 y_2 - \Sigma y_{1c} y_{2c} = 311 \cdot 26$$
$$\Sigma y_2^2 - \Sigma y_{2o}^2 = 933 \cdot 39$$

Secondly, regressing y_1 and y_2 on x_2 alone, we have

$$d_{12}^* = 605 \cdot 39/2023 \cdot 78 = \cdot 2991$$
$$d_{22}^* = 447 \cdot 83/2023 \cdot 78 = \cdot 2213$$
$$\Sigma y_{1c}^{*2} = \cdot 2991 \times 605 \cdot 39 = 191 \cdot 07$$
$$\Sigma y_{1c}^* y_{2c}^* = \cdot 2991 \times 447 \cdot 83$$
$$(\text{or} = \cdot 2213 \times 605 \cdot 39) = 133 \cdot 96$$
$$\Sigma y_{2c}^{*2} = \cdot 2213 \times 447 \cdot 83 = 99 \cdot 10$$

and the second set of residual sums is

$$\Sigma y_1^2 - \Sigma y_{1c}^{*2} = 2294 \cdot 07$$
$$\Sigma y_1 y_2 - \Sigma y_{1c}^* y_{2c}^* = 1238 \cdot 90$$
$$\Sigma y_2^2 - \Sigma y_{2c}^{*2} = 1402 \cdot 76$$

Therefore

$$(2294 \cdot 07 - 460 \cdot 71\lambda)b_{21} + (1238 \cdot 90 - 311 \cdot 26\lambda)(-1) = 0$$
$$(1238 \cdot 90 - 311 \cdot 26\lambda)b_{21} + (1402 \cdot 76 - 933 \cdot 39\lambda)(-1) = 0$$

$$\begin{vmatrix} 2294 \cdot 07 - 460 \cdot 71\lambda & 1238 \cdot 90 - 311 \cdot 26 \\ 1238 \cdot 90 - 311 \cdot 26\lambda & 1402 \cdot 76 - 933 \cdot 39 \end{vmatrix} = 0$$

$$333\,139\lambda^2 - 2\,016\,288\lambda + 1\,683\,156 = 0$$
$$\lambda^2 - 6 \cdot 0524\lambda + 5 \cdot 0524 = 0$$
$$\lambda = 1$$
$$183\,336 b_{21}(\text{LI}) - 927 \cdot 64 = 0$$
$$b_{21}(\text{LI}) = \cdot 5060$$
$$= b_{21}(\text{IL})$$

c_{22} is now estimated by regressing the composite variable $y_2 - b_{21}y_1$ on x_2; that is to say

$$c_{22}(\text{LI}) = [\Sigma x_2 y_2 - b_{21}(\text{LI})\,\Sigma x_2 y_1]/\Sigma x_2^2$$
$$= (447 \cdot 83 - \cdot 5060 \times 605 \cdot 39)/2023 \cdot 78$$
$$= \cdot 0699 = c_{22}(\text{IL})$$

Finally

$$d_{11}(\text{LI}) = \cdot 5147/\cdot 739\,56 = \cdot 6960$$
$$d_{12}(\text{LI}) = \cdot 03598/\cdot 739\,56 = \cdot 0487$$
$$d_{21}(\text{LI}) = \cdot 260\,44/\cdot 739\,56 = \cdot 3522$$
$$d_{22}(\text{LI}) = \cdot 0699/\cdot 739\,56 = \cdot 0945$$

(e) *Full-information maximum likelihood*

Assuming the errors to be independent, the method leads to the following equations:

$$b_{12}\Sigma(y_2 + x_1)^2 + ns_1^2 b_{21}/(1 - b_{12}b_{21}) = \Sigma(y_2 + x_1)y_1$$
$$b_{21}\Sigma y_1^2 + c_{22}\Sigma x_2 y_1 + ns_2^2 b_{12}/(1 - b_{12}b_{21}) = \Sigma y_1 y_2$$
$$b_{21}\Sigma x_2 y_1 + c_{22}\Sigma x_2^2 = \Sigma x_2 y_2$$

and with the given data, noting that $ns_1^2 = \Sigma u_1^2$ and $ns_2^2 = \Sigma u_2^2$

$$8432{\cdot}13b_{12} + b_{21}\Sigma u_1^2/(1 - b_{12}b_{21}) = 4148{\cdot}61$$
$$2475{\cdot}14b_{21} + 605{\cdot}39c_{22} + b_{12}\Sigma u_2^2/(1 - b_{12}b_{21}) = 1372{\cdot}86$$
$$605{\cdot}39b_{21} + 2023{\cdot}78c_{22} = 447{\cdot}83$$

The equations may be solved by an iterative method, starting with $b_{12}(\text{SE})$, $b_{21}(\text{SE})$ and $c_{22}(\text{SE})$, computing the residual sums of squares Σu_1^2 and Σu_2^2, then substituting them in the equations to obtain new coefficient estimates, and so on. After the fifth iteration the results become stabilized with

$$b_{12}(\text{ML}) = {\cdot}4711$$
$$b_{21}(\text{ML}) = {\cdot}3380$$
$$c_{22}(\text{ML}) = {\cdot}1202$$

and therefore

$$d_{11}(\text{ML}) = {\cdot}4711/{\cdot}840\,77 = {\cdot}5603$$
$$d_{12}(\text{ML}) = {\cdot}056\,63/{\cdot}840\,77 = {\cdot}0674$$
$$d_{21}(\text{ML}) = {\cdot}159\,23/{\cdot}840\,77 = {\cdot}1894$$
$$d_{22}(\text{ML}) = {\cdot}1202/{\cdot}840\,77 = {\cdot}1430$$

To summarize, the five sets of estimates are:

	SE	IL	TS	LI	ML
b_{12}	·4920	—	·5117	·5147	·4711
b_{21}	·5400	·5060	·5060	·5060	·3380
c_{22}	·0597	·0699	·0699	·0699	·1202
d_{11}	·6700	·6688	·6905	·6960	·5603
d_{12}	·0400	·2610	·0483	·0487	·0674
d_{21}	·3618	·3384	·3494	·3522	·1894
d_{22}	·0183	·2020	·0943	·0945	·1430

The maximum-likelihood estimates differ substantially from the others, except with regard to the first structural equation; they are not necessarily superior, since their optimal asymptotic properties are of little relevance with a short observation series. The coefficients of x_2 in the estimated reduced form equations are also at variance with the corresponding coefficients derived from the structural equations; this is understandable since the former do not comply with the restrictions which the form of the model imposes. Otherwise, the results of the various methods are very similar.

To revert to the original variables, the constant terms in the regression equations are computed, e.g. with the two-stage least-squares estimates

$$a_1 = \bar{y}_1' - \cdot 5117 \, (\bar{y}_2' + \bar{x}_1')$$
$$= 7 \cdot 690$$
$$a_2 = \bar{y}_2' - \cdot 5060 \, \bar{y}_1' - \cdot 0699 \, \bar{x}_2'$$
$$= 4 \cdot 477$$

and the structural equations in terms of economic variables become

$$Y = 7 \cdot 690 + \cdot 5117 \, (C + D) + u_1$$
$$C = 4 \cdot 477 + \cdot 5060 \, Y + \cdot 0699 \, Y_{-1} + u_2$$

Similarly the reduced-form equations are obtained as

$$Y = 13 \cdot 466 + \cdot 6905 \, D + \cdot 0483 \, Y_{-1} + v_1$$
$$C = 11 \cdot 292 + \cdot 3494 \, D + \cdot 0943 \, Y_{-1} + v_2$$

The structural equations are used for economic interpretation, the reduced-form equations for predictive purposes. For example, for 1962/63

$$Y_{-1} = 56 \cdot 0$$

and the predictions then solely depend on the value inserted for D in the equations

$$Y_p = 16 \cdot 17 + \cdot 6905 \, D$$
$$C_p = 16 \cdot 57 + \cdot 3494 \, D$$

e.g., with $D = 40$, $Y_p = 43 \cdot 8$ and $C_p = 30 \cdot 5$.

4.5 Choice of estimation method

It has been shown that in a recursive system of equations, no real estimation problem arises since single-equation estimators are not only unbiased and consistent but under the usual assumptions even optimal. Indirect least-squares estimation would in this case have neither theoretical nor practical advantages.

In an interdependent system, on the other hand, simultaneous-equation methods yielding consistent estimates of the structural coefficients are generally preferred to single-equation estimates which may have smaller sampling variances but are not consistent. Such a system may, of course, contain equations in which predetermined variables alone appear on the right-hand side; and such equations may be estimated by direct least squares. There may also be some exactly identified equations, and no real difficulty arises in connection with these since the method of indirect least squares provides the obvious solution.

The main estimation problems arise in connection with over-identified equations, which may be all or part of the whole set. Indirect least squares does not yield structural coefficient estimates in this case, and although the reduced-form coefficients may be used for prediction, they are not compatible with the assumptions implied in the model.

The source of the simultaneous equation bias introduced by injudicious use of single-equation least squares lies in the treatment of endogenous variables, which are subject to disturbances, in the same way as predetermined variables. A similar effect was encountered in simple regression when the independent variable was subject to error; and one way of overcoming the bias was to use an instrumental variable. It would seem to follow that in interdependent equation systems too, consistency may be ensured by using suitable instrumental variables in computing the sums of squares and cross products.

This is in fact the case; and the instrumental variables principle provides, in very general terms, a simultaneous equation estimation method. Nor does one have to look very far for instrumental variables, which may be chosen from the predetermined variables and linear combinations thereof. Since an identified equation does not require the estimation of more than k parameters, and an over-identified equation even fewer, such a choice is always practicable. Indeed, both two-stage least squares and limited-information maximum likelihood may be considered as special cases of the instrumental variables method, using prescribed combinations of the predetermined variables arrived at by means of the reduced form equations, and thereby getting over the arbitrary element which the general method possesses.

To look at the matter in a different way, one can also say that both two-stage least-squares and limited information estimation are based on reduced sums of squares and products which have been purged of their error components as far as practicable. In the terminology of Theil (1961), they both form part of the k-class of estimators, which includes inconsistent estimators such as ordinary least squares as well as consistent ones.

Another method is that of three-stage least squares, introduced by Zellner and Theil (1962). The method uses the two-stage least-squares computations but then proceeds to simultaneous estimation of the coefficients in all over-identified equations. This may imply a gain in efficiency and tends to approach full maximum-likelihood estimation closer than does two-stage least squares.

In the methods mentioned and other variants, there is a wide variety of estimation procedures available, the main large-sample properties of which are known. However, in econometric work, the number of observations available is often such that it cannot be described as a large sample, and the behaviour of estimators in small samples is therefore of interest. This is not always easy to establish.

It should also be borne in mind that the basic assumptions of linear regression may not be satisfied in a simultaneous equation system either. There may be errors of measurement in the exogenous variables; the error terms in the equations may be heteroscedastic, or they may be autocorrelated. The last named possibility is particularly serious in view of the fact that lagged endogenous variables are frequently included among the predetermined variables, with the resulting bias which this entails.

Nor can it be taken for granted that all the equations in a model are correctly specified. Possible specification errors include the omission of an important variable or its replacement by an irrelevant one, and a mistaken assumption of linearity where in fact the relationship between the variables is non-linear. These are quite serious possibilities in economics as the exact nature of the relationships is often in doubt.

An extreme view on this matter is taken by Liu (1960). Whilst most econometric models which have been constructed are over-identified, at least in part, Liu argues that in reality the equations would be under-identified if correctly specified, in view of the large number of factors exerting an influence on economic variables. If this argument was accepted, it would logically follow that one should construct and estimate the reduced forms with a large number of predetermined variables, and use these coefficient estimates for prediction.

Against this view, it is contended that economic theory can help in reducing the number of parameters for estimation to essentials, in order to give relationships on which some reliance can be placed. In this sense, correct specification of an equation means the inclusion of all important variables in their correct form; less important variables may be subsumed by the disturbance term. The search for correct specification, which will also minimize the risk of autocorrelated errors, remains an important task in econometrics.

The performance of the diverse estimation methods in various circumstances has been investigated particularly by means of simulation studies, in which sampling experiments are carried out on estimated coefficients in a model with theoretically specified structural equations and coefficients. A specially wide-ranging study of this kind, including estimation after correct and incorrect specification, was made by Summers (1965), using a simple model with two over-identified equations. Ordinary least squares, two-stage least squares, limited information and full maximum likelihood were the methods investigated, together with unrestricted reduced-form estimation in the case of the reduced-form coefficients.

Summers' main findings were that in favourable conditions, full maximum likelihood comes out best and ordinary least squares worst as far as the structural coefficient estimation is concerned. With high correlations between the predetermined variables, however, two-stage least squares appears to be more reliable than either of the maximum-likelihood methods. When a variable is omitted from one of the equations, full-information maximum likelihood gives poor results even for the correctly specified equation whilst the two-stage method performs relatively well. For predictions with the aid of reduced-form coefficients, ordinary least squares again appears inferior to the other methods, the differences between which are not clear-cut.

Another simulation study by Cragg (1967) investigates the estimation of structural coefficients by direct least squares, a further k-class estimator in addition to two-stage least squares and limited information, as well as three-stage least squares and full maximum likelihood. He finds that direct least squares gives rather worse results, and both three-stage least squares and full maximum likelihood rather better results, than the remaining estimators, but that the differences are not very marked. On these grounds he recommends the use of two-stage least squares on grounds of its simplicity and does not rule out the use of ordinary least squares.

The choice of estimation methods may thus be seen in its proper perspective. Whilst some methods are theoretically more satisfying than others, practical considerations may suggest the use of comparatively simple methods such as two-stage least squares. Direct least squares also has its place, if only for the purpose of a preliminary estimation where there is some doubt about the exact model specification and various alternatives are being tried out.

There remains the possibility that a recursive model, and therefore ordinary least squares, may be appropriate in the particular context with which the econometrician is concerned. The use of such models, reflecting a one-way causal chain between the endogenous variables, has been advocated by Wold and his school, for example in Wold and Juréen (1953). There may be less scope for recursive models in the macro-economic field than in, say, demand analysis, but the matter certainly deserves investigation.

There can be no doubt that the simultaneous equation approach has made a powerful contribution to econometrics. It has pointed out the need for proper formulation of relationships and for looking at any one relationship between economic variables in companionship with others which may have a bearing on the variables concerned. It is not denied that in many circumstances it is safe to ignore these additional relationships, and that the application of least squares to a single equation maintains an important place in econometrics.

ANSWERS TO EXERCISES

4.1

$$y_1 = d_{11} x_1 + d_{12} x_2$$
$$y_2 = d_{21} x_1 + d_{22} x_2$$

$$d_{12} + \lambda d_{22} = 0$$
$$\lambda = -d_{12}/d_{22}$$
$$y_1 = (d_{12}/d_{22}) y_2 + (d_{11} - d_{12} d_{21}/d_{22}) x_1$$

$$\lambda' d_{11} + d_{21} = 0$$
$$\lambda' = -d_{21}/d_{11}$$
$$y_2 = (d_{21}/d_{11}) y_1 + (d_{22} - d_{12} d_{21}/d_{11}) x_2$$

Thus $b_{12} = d_{12}/d_{22}$
$$b_{21} = d_{21}/d_{11}$$
$$c_{11} = (d_{11} d_{22} - d_{12} d_{21})/d_{22}$$
$$c_{22} = (d_{11} d_{22} - d_{12} d_{21})/d_{11}$$

4.2 Three variables are excluded from each equation, which suggests exact identification. But the coefficients of the variables excluded from each equation give the determinants:

1st:
$$\begin{vmatrix} 0 & \gamma_{22} & 0 \\ 0 & \gamma_{32} & 0 \\ -1 & 0 & \gamma_{43} \end{vmatrix} = 0$$

2nd:
$$\begin{vmatrix} -1 & 0 & 0 \\ \beta_{31} & 0 & 0 \\ \beta_{41} & -1 & \gamma_{43} \end{vmatrix} = 0$$

3rd:
$$\begin{vmatrix} \beta_{12} & 0 & 0 \\ -1 & 0 & 0 \\ \beta_{42} & -1 & \gamma_{43} \end{vmatrix} = 0$$

4th:
$$\begin{vmatrix} \beta_{13} & \gamma_{11} & 0 \\ \beta_{23} & \gamma_{21} & \gamma_{22} \\ -1 & \gamma_{31} & \gamma_{32} \end{vmatrix} \neq 0$$

71

4.3 $\Sigma xy_2 = 1\,327 \cdot 90 - 1\,429 \cdot 14 = -101 \cdot 24$

$d = -101 \cdot 24/141 \cdot 46 \quad = -\cdot 7157$

$b(RF) = -\cdot 7157/2 \cdot 951 \quad = -\cdot 243$

which is somewhat farther from $\beta = -\cdot 2$ than $b(SE)$.

4.4
$$\Sigma y_{1c}^2 = 2014 \cdot 43$$
$$\Sigma y_{1c}x_2 = 605 \cdot 39$$
$$\Sigma x_2^2 = 2023 \cdot 78$$
$$\Sigma y_{1c}y_2 = 1061 \cdot 60$$
$$\Sigma x_2 y_2 = 447 \cdot 83$$

Hence by regressing y_2 on y_{1c} and x_2

$$b_{21}(TS) = 1\,877\,333/3\,710\,266 = \cdot 5060$$
$$c_{22}(TS) = 259\,440/3\,710\,266 = \cdot 0699$$

PART II: APPLICATIONS

5. PRODUCTION FUNCTIONS

5.1 Theoretical formulation

The concept of the production function is of importance in the theory of the firm, which forms an integral part of economic theory. It is therefore not surprising that the problem of giving quantitative content to the theoretical concept is one that has received a great deal of attention in econometric studies.

In their most general form, production functions are relationships between a number of outputs, or quantities of various products obtained, and a number of inputs, or quantities of factors utilized in production. In this form, however, the problem of obtaining quantitative relationships would be almost intractable. The form of relationship encountered in practical work is therefore frequently of the kind

$$P = g(f_1, \ldots, f_k; \beta_1, \ldots, \beta_n) \tag{5.1}$$

where g is a function containing one or several parameters, P indicates production, and $f_1, \ldots, f_k$ the k factors of production like labour, capital and land. Since linearity in the parameters, though not linearity in the original variables, is required for ordinary estimation, it is an advantage if the relationship can be written as

$$g_0(P) = \alpha + \beta_1 g_1(f_1, \ldots, f_k) + \cdots + \beta_h g_h(f_1, \ldots, f_k) \tag{5.2}$$

where $g_0, g_1, \ldots, g_h$ are mathematical functions of the variables which might be the variables themselves or, for example, their logarithms, but do not contain any parameters to be estimated. This formulation is certainly realistic where there is only one homogeneous product. In cases of joint production, the various outputs have to be combined into a single figure giving value or volume of output for the form of relation to be applicable; also the prices of different products should remain in more or less constant proportions to each other.

This formulation implicitly assumes that factor substitution is possible, i.e. that the factors of production can be combined in different proportions. Furthermore it is assumed that it is not the level of output which is controlled but the input of factors; with each factor combination a certain level of output will result. The simplest mathematical form may appear to be one in which production is a linear function of the factor inputs. This, however, would imply that it is possible to substitute one factor for another at the same rate whatever are the levels of the inputs, and therefore to produce the same quantity by using the cheapest factor only, which is clearly unrealistic. Production functions used in practice, in the case of two factors, are the following.

(a) *Quadratic function*

$$P = \alpha + \beta_1 f_1 + \beta_2 f_2 + \gamma_{11} f_1^2 + 2\gamma_{12} f_1 f_2 + \gamma_{22} f_2^2 \tag{5.3}$$

This gives plausible results provided that

$$\beta_1 > 0 \qquad \beta_2 > 0$$
$$\gamma_{11} < 0 \qquad \gamma_{22} < 0$$
$$\gamma_{12} > 0 \qquad \gamma_{12}^2 < \gamma_{11}\gamma_{22}$$

for the marginal productivity of the first factor is

$$\partial P / \partial f_1 = \beta_1 + 2(\gamma_{11} f_1 + \gamma_{12} f_2)$$

and if the inequalities are satisfied, this expression is positive at input levels, increases with rising f_2 and decreases with rising f_1; similarly for the second factor. Furthermore there exists a theoretical combination of factor inputs which yields maximum output. The production function is then realistic for input levels up to this maximizing combination. There also exists, for any given price situation, a combination of factor inputs which maximizes the net revenue.

(b) *Cobb–Douglas function*

$$\left. \begin{array}{l} P = \alpha' f_1^{\beta_1} f_2^{\beta_2} \\ \log P = \alpha + \beta_1 \log f_1 + \beta_2 \log f_2 \end{array} \right\} \tag{5.4}$$

or

The function could be described as a double-logarithmic or log-linear one but owes its name in this context to its use in the classical production function study by Cobb and Douglas (1928). The parameters β_1 and β_2 may be interpreted as elasticities of output with regard to either of the two factors, i.e. the proportionate increase in P associated with a proportionate increase in f_1 or f_2 alone, leaving the other factor unchanged. Furthermore, there exists, at a given level of output, a factor combination which minimizes costs and thereby maximizes profits.

Exercise 5.1 Writing p_1 and p_2 for the factor prices, derive the optimal ratio of factor inputs and interpret the result.

There are decreasing, constant, or increasing returns to scale

according to whether
$$\beta_1 + \beta_2 \lessgtr 1$$

The function does not allow for the possibility of increasing returns at low levels and decreasing returns at high output levels; hence it does not lend itself to the determination of an optimal scale of production.

The elasticity of substitution σ is defined as
$$\sigma = (r\partial R/\partial r)/R$$
where
$$r = -\mathrm{d}f_2/\mathrm{d}f_1$$

(the marginal rate of substitution).
$$R = f_2/f_1$$

For the Cobb–Douglas function, keeping output constant:
$$f_2 = \text{const.} \times f_1^{-\beta_1/\beta_2}$$
$$r = \beta_1 f_2/\beta_2 f_1$$
$$R = \beta_2 r/\beta_1$$
$$\partial R/\partial r = \beta_2/\beta_1 = R/r$$
$$\sigma = 1$$

The implication is that there exists considerable scope for substitution between factors at any level of output.

(c) *Constant elasticity of substitution (CES) function*
$$P = \gamma[\delta f_1^{-\rho} + (1-\delta)f_2^{-\rho}]^{-\nu/\rho} \tag{5.5}$$

This function was introduced by Arrow, Chenery, Minhas and Solow (1961) for the case $\nu = 1$, representing constant returns to scale, and in its general form by Brown and de Cani (1963). It shares with the Cobb–Douglas function the property of a constant substitution elasticity but covers both the cases $0 < \sigma < 1$ and $\sigma > 1$. For the production isoquants, characterized by constant P, can be written as
$$f_2 = (\alpha_1 - \alpha_2 f_1^{-\rho})^{-1/\rho}$$

where α_1 and α_2 are constants. Hence
$$r = (1/\rho) \times (\alpha_1 - \alpha_2 f_1^{-\rho})^{-(1+\rho)/\rho} \times \alpha_2 \rho f_1^{-(1+\rho)}$$
$$= \alpha_2 (f_2/f_1)^{1+\rho}$$
$$R = \alpha_2^{-1/1+\rho} \, r^{1/1+\rho}$$
$$\partial R/\partial r = (R/r) \times (1/1+\rho)$$
$$\sigma = 1/1+\rho \tag{5.6}$$

Therefore if
$$-1 < \rho < 0: \quad \sigma > 1$$
$$\rho > 1: \quad \sigma < 1$$

The latter case is believed to be of greater importance than the former.

The CES production function does not lend itself to a transformation into the form (5.2). The estimation of its parameters therefore presents more difficult problems than that of the Cobb–Douglas function parameters.

It cannot even be taken for granted that (5.1) is the correct formulation, and other approaches are possible. For example, it may be assumed that for a given industry, the factors of production such as the materials furnished by other industries as well as labour and capital used are in fixed proportion to each other and proportionate to total output of the industry. This is the approach of input–output analysis, in which the emphasis lies on the study of inter-industry relations. It was applied first by Leontief (1951) to the United States and subsequently by other scholars and by statistical bureaux to various countries. Here the parameters are not estimated by regression methods but by *a priori* technical knowledge or by methods of statistical measurement. For this reason, input–output analysis is generally considered a fringe subject of econometrics.

Whilst not going as far as input–output analysis which excludes, at least in its basic form, the possibility of factor substitution, nevertheless it may be appropriate to treat one of the factor inputs rather than output as the dependent variable. It may be assumed, for example, that the remaining factors are fixed in the short run and that the output level is decided upon; the production function then describes a factor requirement. This approach was followed, for example, in a study of short-run employment functions by Wilson and Eckstein (1964).

Alternatively, the production function in its form (5.1) may be supplemented by additional equations specifying optimum factor input levels. If the correct model specification includes these additional equations, their neglect may lead to least-squares bias, and there may even be problems of identification in the making. This was first recognized and pointed out by Marschak and Andrews (1944).

On the other hand, just as the output of different products can be combined into a single index, the input of all factors may likewise be combined into a single cost figure. A bivariate relationship between output and cost is then obtained; it is customary to treat cost as function of output and to speak of a cost function in this context. The cost function may be obtained by substituting the optimal factor combination into the production function; in this sense, the cost function may be said to be derived from the production function.

The estimation of cost functions is facilitated by the use of accounting data in an inter-firm comparison or in a time-series analysis but nevertheless presents some intricate problems. Moreover, it is important in this context not only to estimate parameters but also to test hypotheses regarding the mathematical form of the function, especially in order to ascertain whether the average cost curve is U-shaped or L-shaped.

A pioneering cost function study based on the operations of a furniture factory was made by Dean (1936); the author subsequently was responsible for other studies both by himself and in collaboration. For example, Dean (1942) analysed sales and costs in three departments of a department store, using monthly data covering a period of 5 years (1931–35). A number of variables were tried out for their contribution to the explanation of cost variations, but in the final form of the relationship, only the number of transactions and their average value were included. A quadratic term was retained only for the coat department, whilst purely linear functions were preferred for the hosiery and shoe departments.

A number of empirical studies were also made, and the whole problem surveyed and discussed, by Johnston (1960). The general picture appears to be one of little significant deviation from linearity in the total cost function; there is at any rate insufficient evidence for increasing marginal cost and a U-shaped average cost curve.

5.2 Technical process functions

Production function studies have been made in different fields and with the help of different kinds of data. They may refer to a technical process in industry or agriculture, in which case the variables refer to physical quantities of goods used or produced. Alternatively, they may refer to a particular firm, an industry, an industrial sector or the economy as a whole; in that case, the variables are generally highly aggregated concepts such as labour and capital.

The analysis of technical process data is, within the limitations of its scope, generally straightforward and creates relatively few problems. Such studies have been carried out before production function studies were introduced into economics, for example in agriculture. In this field, much work has been done by Heady and his associates, and a substantial body of results as well as problems encountered is found in Heady and Dillon (1961). For example, the yield of a crop may be treated as a function of the amounts of nitrogen and phosphate applied. In this case, the variables are given, though the omitted variables should be noted. In particular, land is taken as fixed, and the resulting production function will give no information about the effect of different amounts of land for crop production, nor about the use of capital, etc.

Data may be obtained by experiment. This has an advantage over the use of published data, in that as many observations may be obtained as desired; and the explanatory variables can be set at controlled levels. Thus there is little or no danger of multicollinearity, particularly if a simple form of equation, not containing too many parameters, is chosen.

The choice of the mathematical form is generally governed by empirical rather than theoretical considerations here. With a sufficiently wide range of observations, it may well be practicable to test a number of formulae and to ascertain which of them gives a good fit. By increasing the number of parameters the overall fit is of course improved, though the individual coefficients may become less reliable.

A typical result is the production function quoted by Heady and Pesek (1960):

$$Y = -5{\cdot}682 + 6{\cdot}3512\sqrt{N} + 8{\cdot}5155\sqrt{P} - {\cdot}316\,N - {\cdot}417\,P$$
$$+ {\cdot}3410\sqrt{NP}$$

where Y = corn output (bushels per acre),

   N = nitrogen   (lb per acre),

   P = phosphate   (lb per acre).

This can be considered as a variant of the quadratic form if $\sqrt{N}$ and $\sqrt{P}$ are taken as f_1 and f_2 respectively. All the coefficients have the expected sign, and the function is meaningful, as a simple reflection will show.

To interpret the result, it is useful to obtain the partial derivatives $\partial Y/\partial N$ and $\partial Y/\partial P$, showing the additional corn output which the application of an extra lb of nitrogen or of phosphate yields at various levels of factor use.

Exercise 5.2   Derive the factor combination giving the maximum output, and the value of this output.

The existence of such a maximum depends, of course, on the appropriateness of the quadratic form (5.3), and the optimum levels may lie outside the range of the observations, thus being obtained by extrapolation and not being very reliable. Of greater interest are the levels of N and P at which the profit

$$R = \pi Y - p_1 N - p_2 P$$

becomes a maximum, where p_1 and p_2 are the fertilizer prices and π the corn price. Since

$$\partial R/\partial N = \pi \partial Y/\partial N - p_1$$
$$\partial R/\partial P = \pi \partial Y/\partial P - p_2$$

it follows that at the maximum output level, at which

$$\partial Y/\partial N = \partial Y/\partial P = 0$$
$$\partial R/\partial N < 0$$

and
$$\partial R/\partial P < 0$$

Therefore the amount of nitrogen and phosphate which should be applied per acre to yield the best financial returns are less than those giving maximum physical output. Their exact values depend, of course, on the prices in relation to each other.

5.3 Production functions for economic units

The main econometric problem in the field of production functions concerns, in its simplest form, the relationship between output on one hand and both capital and labour used on the other. Additional factors such as land may be introduced into the analysis, and different kinds of capital and labour may be distinguished. Time series or cross section data, referring to different industries, firms within an industry, or different areas may be used for estimation.

Some difficulties in finding suitable data are frequently encountered. A volume index of production may be available, or it may have to be obtained as a deflated value with the help of a price index. Labour is perhaps best indicated by number of man-hours spent in production, but the number of workers employed may have to be used. The measurement of capital presents particular difficulties since no officially published data may be available even for the value of capital in existence. As a preliminary measure to the econometric analysis it is therefore frequently necessary for the investigator to estimate capital stock from past investment and, in the case of time series, to convert it from money terms into real terms.

The original study by Cobb and Douglas (1928) concerned itself with manufacturing as a whole in the United States, and annual data from 1899 to 1922 furnished the basis of observation. Estimates of the average number of wage-earners employed and total fixed capital in 1880 dollars were used together with a volume of production index. Assuming constant returns to scale and therefore a sum of 1 for the coefficients of the two variables, the production function obtained was

$$\log P = \text{const.} + \cdot 75 \log L + \cdot 25 K + u$$

In a subsequent investigation by Douglas (1934) various modifications were introduced by revising the data, dropping the assumption of constant returns, and eliminating the time trend. The resulting elasticities with regard to labour vary between ·63 and ·90, and those for capital between ·10 and ·31.

The original result has been widely quoted and has been claimed to be of wide applicability, though with appropriate modifications in each case. Confirmation of this view may be derived from the fact that on the basis of theoretical considerations the two elasticities may be expected also to represent the shares of labour and capital in the distribution of income, and that these shares are indeed observed to be in the neighbourhood of ·75 and ·25 respectively.

This interpretation of the results has, however, been queried, notably by Mendershausen (1938) who pointed out that instead of regressing $\log P$ on $\log L$ and $\log K$, it would be quite appropriate to construct regressions of $\log L$, $\log K$ and $\log P$ on time t. The coefficients ·75 and ·25 then may be said merely to represent ratios of differences between the slopes of the trend lines.

Exercise 5.3 Show that with the data of Example 3.2, this interpretation would be reasonable.

Criticism directed towards the Cobb–Douglas approach has been concerned with the highly aggregative nature of the data which conceals important changes in the structure of manufacturing, with the use of time series and the interpretation of results derived from them, and more recently with the mathematical form of the Cobb–Douglas function and its implication of unit elasticity of substitution. These points have been met, at least partially, by subsequent production function studies, some of them being carried out by Douglas and his associates.

Studies for individual industries using time-series data are, for example, those for agriculture and coal mining in the United Kingdom by Lomax (1949, 1950). For coal mining, the elasticities found are ·79 with regard to labour and ·29 with regard to capital, accompanied by a negative time trend; similar results are obtained by a geographical cross section study. For agriculture, additional variables considered but finally excluded were land as well as fertilizers and feeding stuffs; a time trend was also introduced which turned out to be positive. The elasticities were found to be ·37 for capital but only ·18 for labour, and therefore quite different from the results of Cobb and Douglas, whilst the figures for coal mining are in good agreement with them.

The cross-section studies undertaken by Douglas and his school were in the nature of inter-industry comparisons. In the first of these, presented by Bronfenbrenner and Douglas (1939), data for 90 manufacturing industries in the 1909 U.S. Census of Manufacturers were utilized, and regressions using either total or fixed capital were calculated for all industries as well as some subsets obtained when the industries were classified by degree of capital intensity or by industry group. For all industries, the elasticities for capital and labour are ·74 and ·32 respectively when total capital is used but ·86 and ·08 with fixed capital.

A number of inter-industry cross section studies, as well as some time-series studies, for the United States and other countries, were surveyed by Douglas (1948). The results generally indicate output elasticities with regard to labour lying between ·5 and ·75, and elasticities with regard to capital between ·25 and ·5. Where the coefficients are separately estimated, their sum rarely differs significantly from unity, and the hypothesis of constant returns to scale is not disproved. The inter-industry comparisons therefore appear to corroborate the findings derived from time series.

However, inter-industry studies lay themselves open to objections on theoretical grounds which may be even weightier than those against time-series studies. For one thing, output data are given in monetary units and the results therefore reflect variations not only in quantity but also in price. Moreover, the implicit assumption that all industries have similar production functions is necessary for the derivation of results but may not be realistic. On these grounds, findings derived from inter-industry comparisons are of less interest than those of other cross section studies.

The use of international or inter-regional data appears to be more promising. It is true that the analysis depends on the choice of the exchange rate in international comparisons, and that industries in different countries or areas may have different product mixes though statistically classified in the same way. However, some studies of this kind, based both on individual industries and on large economic sectors, have been undertaken.

An ambitious attempt to relate international differences in real national income to differences in labour, capital and land was made by Olson (1948). Data for 24 countries in or around 1937 were used, capital K being represented by total non-human energy used or alternatively by two variables, the second one (K') being livestock units. The coefficient of land was found to be positive in the regression without livestock and negative with the full set of variables but in neither case statistically significant. The preferred equation therefore was

$$\log P = ·23 \log L + ·50 \log K + ·28 \log K' + u$$

which indicates constant returns to scale but points to capital playing a dominant role in explaining international differences in living standards, in contrast to the usual production function results.

Another approach again proceeds through the medium of inter-firm comparisons. A practical difficulty lies in the fact that data for individual enterprises may be difficult to procure, Census of Production data generally being disclosed for groups of establishments only. A theoretical problem arises out of the fact that prices and other external factors can generally be assumed to be the same for all firms; and if they all adopted the optimal factor combination, the observations would not offer a basis for ascertaining the effect of variations in the ratio of capital to labour. It must therefore be assumed that imperfections of knowledge or of market conditions make for different degrees of efficiency in production.

As against these difficulties, there is the advantage that the number of firms or productive units which provide the basis of observation may run into hundreds, thus giving a large number of degrees of freedom for the statistical analysis. A large number of variables may therefore be introduced without incurring an undue risk of multicollinearity, and a moderate disaggregation of factors is possible.

Econometric inter-firm production studies have notably been undertaken in the field of agriculture. Pioneering studies for American farms were those of Tintner and Brownlee (1944) and Heady (1946); numerous further results are quoted by Heady and Dillon (1961). In the industrial sphere, a detailed investigation was undertaken by Murti and Sastry (1957) for Indian industries.

Tintner (1944) analysed 609 records of farms in Iowa for their operations in 1942. Six factors were distinguished: land, labour, improvements, liquid assets, working assets, and cash expenses. The meaning of the variables is as follows:

Product: Gross profit
Land: Number of acres used
Labour: Months of hired and family labour
Improvements: Fences and buildings
Liquid assets: Livestock, feed, seeds and fertilizers
Working assets: Breeding cattle, horses, tractors, machinery and trucks
Cash operating expenses: Equipment repairs, fuel, oil, purchased feed, etc.

With such a large number of variables, it is natural to take a comparatively simple function, and the Cobb–Douglas form was used. The regression coefficients obtained may thus be directly interpreted as

82

elasticities of output with regard to the various factors. The following elasticities were obtained by Tintner:

Land:	·288
Labour:	·158
Improvements:	·054
Liquid assets:	·212
Working assets:	− ·005
Cash operating expenses:	·159

The negative elasticity for working assets may appear paradoxical, but the figure is, of course, not significantly different from zero. The remaining elasticities are all significantly positive at the 5 per cent level.

If improvements, liquid assets and working assets are counted as capital, then the estimated elasticity of output with regard to all capital is $·054 + ·212 − ·005 = ·261$. This result is in good agreement with results obtained by Douglas and his associates for industry on the basis of time-series and inter-industry data.

Furthermore, the elasticity with regard to all factors is obtained as ·866. This suggests decreasing returns to scale, i.e. relatively less profitable results for larger farms or farms using more land and other resources The difference from unity may, however, be subjected to a significance test, and it is found to be not significant even at the 1 per cent level. The hypothesis of constant returns to scale is thus not contradicted by the study.

Whilst the Cobb–Douglas form of the production function is frequently employed, later studies are based to an increasing extent upon the CES function (5.5). Its use is particularly motivated by the desire to test the hypothesis of unit substitution elasticity instead of assuming it implicitly.

Since the CES function does not lend itself to ordinary least-squares estimation, various estimation methods have been devised. Basically they fall into two categories according to whether they use additional relationships or linear approximations. For example, in the case of constant returns to scale the function is

$$P = \gamma\{\delta L^{-\rho} + (1-\delta)K^{-\rho}\}^{-1/\rho}$$

Given the product price π, wage rate w and interest rate i, net revenue R is

$$R = V - wL - iK \qquad (V = \pi P)$$

and this is maximized when

$$\partial V/\partial L = w$$
$$\partial V/\partial K = i$$

Since $\quad \partial V/\partial L = \text{const.} \times \{\partial L^{-\rho} + (1-\delta)K^{-\rho}\}^{-(1+\rho)/\rho}L^{-(1+\rho)}$
$$= \text{const.} \times (V/L)^{1+\rho}$$

the first of the two equations becomes

$$(V/L)^{1+\rho} = \text{const.} \times w$$

and from (5.6)

$$V/L = \text{const.} \times w^{\sigma}$$
$$\log(V/L) = \text{const.} + \sigma \log w$$

Regression of output per head on the wage rate therefore yields an estimate of the substitution elasticity, or may be used to test the significance of its difference from 1.

Exercise 5.4 Show that with the Cobb–Douglas specification, the corresponding equation is

$$\log(V/L) = \text{const.} + \log w$$

This method was followed by Arrow, Chenery, Minhas and Solow (1961), who used international cross section data for individual industries and generally found the elasticity of substitution to be significantly below 1. The method has been applied to other types of data and has been subject to modifications. Moroney (1970) argues that the use of profit-maximizing equations leads to specification errors and that a cost-minimizing equation is preferable. Estimates of substitution elasticities based on inter-state data for U.S. manufacturing industries in 1957–58, derived by the original method and lying around 1, are suggested to be upward biased; the revised method leads to elasticities which are substantially below 1.

A different method, due to Kmenta (1967), uses the production function itself, which may be written as

$$P/L = \gamma\{\delta + (1-\delta)(K/L)^{-\rho}\}^{-1/\rho}$$

hence $\quad \log(P/L) = \log\gamma\,\{\log[\delta + (1-\delta)(K/L)^{-\rho}]\}/\rho$

and by expanding into a series and neglecting terms of higher order, this may be written as

$$\log(P/L) = \log\gamma + (1-\delta)\log(K/L) - \{\rho\delta(1-\delta)[\log K/L]^2\}/2$$

so that a quadratic regression of $\log P/L$ on $\log K/L$ permits a significance test for the difference of ρ from 0 and therefore that of σ from 1. The values of ρ and the other parameters may be estimated subsequently.

Griliches and Ringstad (1971) applied this method to an analysis of the Norwegian 1963 Census of Manufacturing Establishments, which permitted an inter-firm comparison for a number of industries. The authors do not find any clear indication which would point to an elasticity of substitution different from 1, and therefore conclude that there is no clear evidence for rejecting the Cobb–Douglas function. On the other hand, there appears to be evidence of small but significant economies of scale.

5.4 Measurement of technical progress

When a production function is fitted to time series of output, labour and capital, the growth in production is attributed to the increased use of labour and capital; or we can say that the growth in output per head is ascribed to the increased capital intensity of production and possibly to a scale effect. The question then arises whether other forces such as technical innovations or greater managerial and operative skill should not be credited with part of the achievement. This problem has, understandably enough, received wide attention by theoretical and applied economists.

In theory, it should be possible to isolate the effects of the two kinds of forces upon economic growth by means of partial regression analysis. If the effect of technological changes can be assumed to follow an exponential trend, it may be introduced through time as a variable besides $\log L$ and $\log K$ or their difference in a log-linear function, thereby obtaining the model

$$\log P = \alpha + \beta_1 \log L + \beta_2 \log K + \beta_3 t + \varepsilon \qquad (5.7)$$

Attempts in this direction have indeed been made. Aukrust (1959) analysed Norwegian data for the years 1900–39 and 1946–55 with L representing employment in man-years, K real capital at depreciated replacement cost and P real national product, all data referring to the economy as a whole. The resulting equation was

$$\log P = 2\cdot262 + \cdot763 \log L + \cdot203 \log K + \cdot0181 t + u$$

with standard errors $\cdot101$, $\cdot192$ and $\cdot0029$ respectively for the regression coefficients, and all logarithms being to base e. The values of the elasticities are close to those obtained by Cobb–Douglas, but in addition there is an autonomous increase in output by 1·8 per cent per annum, explaining more than half of the post-war growth rate of 3·4 per cent.

Not all the studies of this kind yielded plausible results. For example, in fitting a production function to manufacturing and mining in the United States between 1920 and 1940, Wall (1948) obtained elasticities of 1·34 and ·93 respectively with regard to labour and capital together with a linear trend, or 1·46 and ·49 together with a quadratic trend; the implied scale effect is not acceptable. Results of this kind may be explained by multicollinearity or by deficiencies in the data. In particular, the influence of capital may not be accurately assessed, since it is virtually impossible to get precise data showing the amount of capital in actual use, and the total capital stock in existence has to be used instead.

In order to separate the effects of capital investment and of technical progress, additional relationships are sometimes used. This device, which was used to overcome non-linearity problems in connection with the CES function, is employed here in a more general context to overcome data limitations.

Solow (1957) uses the following general model, which does not specify the form of the production function proper:

$$\log P(t) = \log A(t) + \log f\{L(t), K(t)\}$$

Denoting derivations with regard to time by $\dot{P}$, $\dot{L}$ and $\dot{K}$, we have

$$\dot{P}/P = \dot{A}/A + \{(\partial f/\partial L)\dot{L} + (\partial f/\partial K)\dot{K}\}/f$$

Assuming constant returns to scale, the elasticities of f with regard to L and K can be taken as equating the shares w_L of labour and w_K of capital in the product ($w_L + w_K = 1$). Hence

$$\dot{A}/A = \dot{P}/P - w_L\dot{L}/L - w_K\dot{K}/K$$

Or, writing $P = pL$ and $K = kL$

$$\dot{A}/A = \dot{p}/p + \dot{L}/L - (1 - w_K)\dot{L}/L - w_K(\dot{k}/k + \dot{L}/L)$$
$$= \dot{p}/p - w_K\dot{k}/k$$

Replacing the derivatives by discrete approximations, the function A, which exhibits the shifts in the production function over time, may be derived from data for output and capital per head or man-hour, and the share of capital. Subsequently the production function may be specified and its parameters estimated.

Solow analyses data for the non-agricultural sector of the United States economy over the period 1909–49, during which output per head increased by 105 per cent. The findings are that technical progress accounts for an increase of 81 per cent, or 1·5 per cent a year on the average, and therefore the increase in capital per head accounts only for a minor part of the economic growth.

86

Another method was used by Johansen (1961), who shows that under certain assumptions, the constant term in a regression of labour productivity increase between two dates on the share of capital in value added may be interpreted as the shift in the production function and therefore the effect of technical progress. With the help of cross section data for 28 British industries in 1924 and 1950, the shift in the production function may be estimated without any capital stock data being required. The figure arrived at is a 20 per cent increase in production over this period, or ·7 per cent per annum, on account of technical progress. Investment, however, also plays a major role here, inducing growth to the tune of 36 per cent between 1924 and 1950.

In the studies mentioned so far, it has been assumed that technical progress may be represented by a multiplicative trend which can be separated from the production function proper. In terms of economic theory, this implies that the progress is neutral in the sense used by Hicks, and in other senses as well if the production function has the Cobb–Douglas form. Technical progress of this kind can be said to be both labour-saving and capital-saving. It is possible to modify this assumption and to introduce non-neutral technological progress into the analysis.

It has been shown that it is not necessary to assume a Cobb–Douglas form of the production function in order to study technical progress; indeed, it is possible to do so by using simple productivity indices. Nevertheless, econometric analyses have brought a substantial stimulus to the study of the problem, and this has been further reinforced by the use of the CES function. In (5.5), changes in the parameter γ indicate neutral progress, but non-neutral progress may also be introduced by means of changes in the parameter δ. For example, an increase in δ may be described as labour-saving, or as labour-augmenting in the sense that the same amount of labour will have greater efficiency.

Non-neutral technical progress may be evaluated if there is no neutral technical progress at the same time. If, however, one attempts to estimate a production function with both kinds of progress being present, then one comes up against identification problems, and estimation is impossible without additional assumptions. Brown and de Cani (1963) estimate production functions for several epochs within the observation period and obtain estimates of technical progress by comparison. They find structural changes in the production function for the U.S. between 1890–1918, 1919–37 and 1938–58; the earlier change is described as predominantly labour-saving, the later change as predominantly capital-saving.

A further assumption which has been implicitly made consists in seeing technological change as disembodied, i.e. continuing at the same rate irrespective of the level of investment and requiring no capital equipment for its realization. In contrast, some or all technical progress may be thought to be embodied in new investment goods produced in a particular year. This argument leads to a vintage model, in which output does not depend merely on size of capital stock, together with labour and time, but on the way the capital stock is made up from capital goods of different vintages. To make this theoretical scheme operational for estimation raises difficulties, not least among them those of procuring adequate data.

Griliches (1963) goes further, in a way, by suggesting that technical progress may be embodied in labour as well as capital. He argues that it is unsatisfactory to obtain technical change as a residual after elimination of the contributions to growth of output made by increase in factor uses, and that in fact most of the residual may be ascribed to specific causes when the variables are correctly measured. In a study of U.S. agriculture between 1940 and 1960, conventional analysis is said to ignore quality improvements in capital and labour, in the latter case indicated by better education, to disregard economies of scale and to give biased results for the elasticities on account of incorrect weighting. When allowance has been made for these deficiencies in data and their use, most of the change in output can be explained without having to call upon a residual.

The field of production function studies has been surveyed wholly or partly by Walters (1963), Brown (1966) and Nerlove (1967). It becomes evident that the topic, which at one time appeared to lend itself to a straightforward analysis, may lead to quite intricate questions which cannot be answered in a simple fashion. The correct interpretation of any results obtained, bearing in mind the adopted specification of the production function relationship, calls for particular attention.

ANSWERS TO EXERCISES

5.1

$$p_1 f_1 + p_2 f_2 - \lambda f_1^{\beta_1} f_2^{\beta_2} = \text{Min.}$$
$$p_i = \lambda P \beta_i / f_i \qquad (i = 1, 2)$$
$$f_2 / f_1 = \beta_2 p_2 / \beta_1 p_2$$

The amounts used of each factor are therefore proportionate to the elasticity of output and inversely proportionate to its price.

$$\partial Y/\partial N = -\cdot316+(3\cdot1756+\cdot1705\sqrt{P})/\sqrt{N}$$
$$\partial Y/\partial P = -\cdot417+(4\cdot2578+\cdot1705\sqrt{N})/\sqrt{P}$$
$$\cdot3160\sqrt{N}-\cdot1705\sqrt{P} = 3\cdot1756$$
$$-\cdot1705\sqrt{N}+\cdot4170\sqrt{P} = 4\cdot2578$$
$$\sqrt{N} = 8\cdot20069/\cdot410807 = 19\cdot962$$
$$\sqrt{P} = 7\cdot54756/\cdot410807 = 18\cdot373$$
$$N = 398\cdot48$$
$$P = 337\cdot67$$
$$Y = 135\cdot9$$

$$\log L = \alpha_1 + \beta_1 t + \varepsilon_1$$
$$\log K = \alpha_2 + \beta_2 t + \varepsilon_2$$
$$\log P = \alpha_3 + \beta_3 t + \varepsilon_3$$
$$b_1 = 1\cdot841/60 = \cdot0307$$
$$b_2 = 3\cdot242/60 = \cdot0540$$
$$b_3 = 2\cdot201/60 = \cdot0367$$
$$r_1^2 = \cdot056519/\cdot056736 = \cdot9962$$
$$r_2^2 = \cdot175068/\cdot175998 = \cdot9947$$
$$r_3^2 = \cdot080777/\cdot082017 = \cdot9849$$

All variables are highly correlated with time.

$$(b_2-b_3)/(b_2-b_1) = \cdot0173/\cdot0233 = \cdot742$$
$$(b_3-b_1)/(b_2-b_1) = \cdot0060/\cdot0233 = \cdot258$$

These values are almost the same as the elasticities in the estimated relationship

$$\log P = \text{const.} + \cdot740 \log L + \cdot260 \log K = u$$

$$V = \pi\alpha L^\beta K^{1-\beta}$$
$$\partial V/\partial L = \beta V/L$$
$$R = V - wL - iK$$
$$\partial R/\partial L = 0$$
$$\beta V/L = w$$
$$\log(V/L) = \log(1/\beta) + \log w$$

6. DEMAND ANALYSIS

6.1 Demand functions and elasticities

The notion of demand for a commodity is familiar not only to the theoretical economist but also to the practical businessman. A producer or retailer may know the existing demand for a product, but the future demand in various circumstances will be a matter of great concern to him; the same applies when the potential demand for a new product is assessed.

The concept of demand also figures prominently in economic theory and analysis, though with a somewhat different emphasis. The businessman is concerned not only with the total market for the commodity he produces or sells but also with the share of the market held by his particular brand; and much of market research is devoted to the question how to maintain or increase a market share. In economics, demand analysis is chiefly or exclusively concerned with the demand for a commodity irrespective of brand, or for a group of commodities like meat or dairy products or, on a higher level of aggregation, for all food, housing, or clothing.

The econometric problem consists in constructing numerical relationships between the demand for a commodity or commodities and the factors which influence the demand. Such a relationship may be called a demand function or, more precisely, a statistical demand function, in contrast to purely theoretical ones. Factors influencing demand obviously include the price of the commodity and the income of the group of consumers under consideration. Other, less obvious, possible factors include: the price of a substitute for the commodity; the general price level; the distribution of income; the stock of the commodity held by the consumers; presence or absence of hire purchase regulations. It is, of course, not necessary for all these factors to enter a particular demand function.

Of particular interest are income and price elasticities of demand which may, for practical purposes, be said to represent the percentage increase or decrease in demand which accompanies a 1 per cent increase in income, or a 1 per cent increase in price. Denoting demand by q, income by Y, and price by p, the demand relationship expresses q as a function of Y, p, and possibly some other variables. The income elasticity Eq/EY and the price elasticity Eq/Ep are then defined as follows:

$$Eq/EY = (Y\partial q/\partial Y)/q$$
$$Eq/Ep = (p\partial q/\partial p)/q \qquad (6.1)$$

The main advantage of discussing demand in terms of elasticities is that these are independent of the units of measurement; thus results are comparable even if derived for countries with different currencies or where the commodities are measured in different physical units. Demand elasticities are not necessarily constants as their value at different price and income levels may differ; but experience shows that it is often legitimate to treat them as approximately constant within a moderately wide range of the variables.

If prices of other commodities appear in the demand function, then one has to distinguish between direct price elasticities with regard to the commodity's own price, and cross price elasticities with regard to other commodities' prices. Theoretically, prices of all commodities entering the customer's budget could enter into the demand function for any commodity. With n commodities, the quantities consumed and prices of which are $q_1, ..., q_n$; $p_1, ..., p_n$ respectively, the scheme of elasticities for the ith commodity is

$$Eq_i/EY = (Y\partial q_i/\partial Y)/q_i$$
$$Eq_i/Ep_i = (p_i \partial q_i/\partial p_i)/q_i$$
$$Eq_i/Ep_i = (p_j \partial q_i/\partial p_j)/q_i \qquad (j \neq i) \qquad (6.2)$$

Nevertheless, the interest generally centres on income and direct price elasticities. It is clear that usually

$$Eq_i/EY > 0$$
$$Eq_i/Ep_i < 0$$

In earlier work, Eq_i/Ep_i was often defined with the opposite sign and therefore usually positive. This practice has been abandoned since cross price elasticities came to be introduced into demand analysis.

Commodities may be classified according to the value of their price or income elasticity of demand. Demand is said to be, with regard to income,

Inelastic if $Eq_i/EY < 1$

Elastic if $Eq_i/EY > 1$

and with regard to own price

Inelastic if $Eq_i/Ep_i > -1$

Elastic if $Eq_i/Ep_i < -1$

Alternatively, a good is said to be

91

$$\text{Inferior if } Eq_i/EY < 0$$
$$\text{A necessity if } 0 < Eq_i/EY < 1$$
$$\text{A luxury if } 1 < Eq_i/EY$$

The theoretical framework from which demand functions and demand elasticities are derived is the theory of consumer's demand based on the notion of the utility function. The basic idea is to consider simultaneously all purchases made within a unit of time; these in combination yield a certain degree of satisfaction to the consumer, depending only on the quantities purchased. Simple and plausible postulates are made about the utility function and about the behaviour of the consumer, who is assumed to maximize his satisfaction subject to his budget restraint. Some important properties are deduced for the demand functions and elasticities.

One difficulty is that the theory, in its initial stages at least, deals with the individual consumer or household whilst econometric analysis studies a group of consumers. The transition from individual to community raises difficult aggregation problems. Under certain assumptions it is possible to assume the existence of a utility function for the community and thus to treat it like an individual consumer.

It is assumed in demand theory that the commodity purchases are made with a view to satisfying wants which the consumer has. This does not apply to intermediate goods used in the production process or investment goods which are bought by producers for the purpose of producing other goods and receiving a monetary reward. Such producers' goods are thus not covered by demand theory but rather by the theory of the firm, and ordinary demand analysis cannot be applied to them. A classical example is the attempt made by Moore (1914) to derive a demand function for pig iron, the price coefficient in which was found to be positive, thus apparently indicating that the higher the price the greater the quantity purchased. The result may be interpreted in terms of a supply function; the identification problem applies here.

A demand analysis may be made for producers' goods, but the fact that they are not directly consumed must be taken into account when specifying the equations and the variables appearing therein. The account given here will be confined to studies of consumer's demand.

6.2 Analysis of household budgets

The two main sources of information utilized for demand studies are household budgets and market data. They may be used separately or in combination. Market data, i.e. published statistics of quantities purchased, prices paid, and other variables are usually time-series, though of course they may also refer to different areas. Household budget collections are the result of special enquiries, almost invariably made on a voluntary and sample basis. In most countries, household budget studies are not made at regular intervals but only intermittently, and their analysis is thus for the most part a cross-section study.

One advantage which household budget studies offer lies in the possibility of analysing all types of expenditure at the same time. Furthermore, within the data published for one period, prices may be taken as constant, as regional price variations can generally be neglected. This limits the analysis, as it means that the effects of price changes cannot be ascertained and income elasticities of demand only can be derived. On the other hand, this very limitation facilitates the analysis to a considerable extent as it drastically reduces the number of variables which have to be introduced and the number of parameters to be estimated.

The analysis may be made on the basis of the individual records, but more often starts from published averages for various groups of households. Provided the grouping is sufficiently fine and there are sufficient cross-classifications, the practical convenience of using the group averages generally more than outweighs the loss of information entailed by this procedure.

The dependent variables in the demand equations are usually expenditure data of the type $v_i = p_i q_i$, sometimes converted into shares of income or total expenditure. Value data are used because quantities are not recorded, and indeed would be difficult to measure, in the case of services and other expenditure categories containing a heterogeneous collection of goods. For foodstuffs and a number of other commodities, household budget enquiries commonly give quantity as well as value data. Theoretically both sets of data should yield the same result for income elasticities since

$$Ev_i/EY = (Yp_i \partial q_i/\partial Y)/p_i q_i$$
$$= Eq_i/EY$$

In practice, the results generally differ because physical quantities are recorded which do not allow for quality variations. With the help of these data, value elasticities may therefore be split up into quantity and quality components.

The chief independent variable is income or an indicator of income. Theoretically one would like to use permanent income or permanent total expenditure, in the sense of Friedman (1957). If Friedman's permanent income hypothesis is correct, the ratio between these two magnitudes does not vary with income, and it follows that income elasticities and total expenditure elasticities are equal. In practice,

93

however, neither of these two concepts is measurable, and actual disposable income or actual total expenditure must be used.

In many household budget collections, information on income has not been sought or could not be obtained accurately, and total outlay is the only possible choice. This may, however, be the better bet even if income data are available, since the use of actual income introduces a downward bias into regression coefficients and income elasticities. The bias arises from the fact that households with high incomes include those benefiting from a temporary windfall, which may not be matched by correspondingly high spending; conversely, households with low incomes include those suffering from a temporary reduction in earning power and therefore dissaving.

The use of actual total outlay may also entail bias owing to abnormal purchases of consumer durables in the survey period; the coefficients and elasticities for durables are then over-estimated and those for non-durables under-estimated. This point has been discussed in detail by Liviatan (1961). A remedy consists in using income as instrumental variable in the regression of commodity expenditure on total expenditure. The model then is

$$y = \beta x_p + x_t + \varepsilon_t$$
$$x = x_p + x_t$$
$$z = \lambda x_p + z_t$$

where y, x and z represent the deviations from mean of durable goods expenditure, total expenditure and income respectively, x_p permanent expenditure, x_t and z_t transitory components. Using ordinary least squares and instrumental variables respectively we obtain

$$b_x = \Sigma xy/\Sigma x^2$$
$$b_z = \Sigma zy/\Sigma zx$$

Assuming x_p, x_t, z_t and ε_t to be uncorrelated with each other we find that, with $0 < \beta < 1$

$$E(b_x) = (\beta \Sigma x_p^2 + \Sigma x_t^2)/(\Sigma x_p^2 + \Sigma x_t^2) > \beta$$
$$E(b_z) = \beta \lambda \Sigma x_p^2/\lambda \Sigma x_p^2 = \beta$$

In practice, the result of the instrumental variables technique may be achieved by using data for household income groups as observations for regression of commodity expenditure on total outlay.

It will be assumed in the following that total expenditure C is used as indicator of income, and that the dependent variables are the amounts spent v_i or their budget shares $w_i = v_i/C$. Then by definition

$$\left.\begin{array}{l} \sum_i v_i = C \\ \sum_i w_i = 1 \end{array}\right\} \tag{6.3}$$

where the summation is taken over all commodities or commodity groups entering household expenditure.

Such demand relationships are usually described as Engel functions, after the German statistician who first made a systematic study of the topic in 1857; an accessible version of the original study is the article by Engel (1895). The exact mathematical formulation of the Engel functions presents another problem.

A simple formulation is provided by the linear Engel function of Allen and Bowley (1935)

$$v_i = \alpha_i + \beta_i C + \varepsilon_i \tag{6.4}$$

Coefficient estimates a_i and b_i are obtained by least squares. If this is done for all commodities, then

$$\sum_i b_i = \Sigma (C-\bar{C})^2 / \Sigma (C-\bar{C})^2 = 1$$
$$\sum_i a_i = \bar{C} - \bar{C} = 0$$

and the theoretical expenditure totals satisfy the relations (6.3). This Engel function is therefore said to satisfy the additivity criterion. The theoretical income elasticities vary slowly with total expenditure; at average level of total outlay

$$\overline{Ev_i}/EC = b_i/\bar{w}_i$$

The demand is therefore inelastic or elastic according to whether

$$b_i \lessgtr \bar{w}_i$$

or $\qquad\qquad\qquad a_i \gtrless 0$

Another simple and widely used form may, after transformation to logarithms, be written as

$$\log v_i = \alpha_i + \beta_i \log C + \varepsilon_i \tag{6.5}$$

in which the elasticities are constant and represented by β_i or their estimates b_i. The constancy of the elasticities is a great practical advantage, but a drawback is that the function does not possess the additivity property.

The function may be modified to meet the additivity criterion. One way of achieving this is by estimating differences between pairs of coefficients (β_i, β_j) and (α_i, α_j) and substituting the results with an arbitrary constant into the expressions

$$v_{ic} = a_i C^{b_i} / \sum_j a_j C^{b_j-1}$$

Alternatively, an additive approximation to (6.5) is provided by the function used by H. Working (1943)

$$w_i = \alpha_i + \beta_i \log C + \varepsilon_i \tag{6.6}$$

In this function, the errors in amounts spent are assumed to be heteroscedastic and increasing with total expenditure, but the errors in budget shares homoscedastic, which seems plausible.

Exercise 6.1 Show that the average income elasticities in model (6.6) are

$$\overline{Ev_i}/EC = 1 + b_i/\bar{w}_i$$

What does the sign of b_i indicate?

Another approach is an application of the log-normal distribution, discussed in detail by Aitchison and Brown (1957). This assumes the existence of various saturation levels for various goods and has theoretically attractive features, though estimation of the sigmoid Engel curves to which the method leads is more laborious than that of the simple functions discussed above.

Of course, the simple formulations assume that apart from a random error term, total expenditure is the only thing that influences the expenditure pattern. This may be realistic if it is possible to divide the population into strata which are fairly homogeneous except with regard to income; simple regression equations can then be fitted to each stratum, or dummy variables may be used. Alternatively, additional variables may be introduced, the most important one being an indicator of family size. Rather than using total number of persons, efforts have been made to find scales by which children of different ages can be converted into equivalent persons. As Forsyth (1960) has pointed out, it is quite difficult to get a satisfactory single indicator of this sort.

In interpreting the results, it is legitimate to speak about income elasticities of demand even though total expenditure is the variable in the regression. Care should, however, be taken not to apply the results of a cross-section study mechanically in a dynamic sense. An income elasticity of ·6 for food means, broadly speaking, that households with 10 per cent higher income spend 6 per cent more on food than households without the extra income. It does not necessarily follow that a

10 per cent increase in family income would invariably be accompanied by a 6 per cent increase in food expenditure.

Most of the theoretical problems which arise in household budget analysis have been investigated and discussed by Prais and Houthakker (1971). This classical work at the same time analyses the results of an official collection of working-class budgets and an unofficial collection of middle-class budgets.

Household budget data have been collected and analysed in a number of countries. Allen and Bowley (1935) surveyed and summarized the results of numerous enquiries. Another comparative study was made by Houthakker (1957), who fits a double-logarithmic function

$$\log v_i = \alpha_i + \beta_i \log C + \gamma_i \log N + \varepsilon_i \tag{6.7}$$

where N represents number of persons, to 31 budget collections and 4 combinations of surveys for 17 different countries, with regard to expenditure on all food, clothing, housing (including fuel and light), and miscellaneous items. The estimates b_i for the income elasticities β_i obtained range from ·34 to ·73 for food, from ·92 to 1·78 for clothing, from ·35 to 1·12 for housing and from 1·08 to 1·88 for miscellaneous items.

Thus the income elasticity for food appears to be invariably below one; or in other words, the share of food expenditure declines with rising total outlay. This empirically established rule, which appears to hold almost universally, is known as Engel's law. It does not exclude the possibility of income elasticities above 1 for particular foodstuffs; such high values were indeed obtained by Allen and Bowley (1935) for meat in 22, for dairy products in 14, and for vegetables in 17 out of 26 surveys analysed.

For housing, an elasticity below 1 is also claimed by " Schwabe's law ". This, however, is much less firmly established than Engel's law. If the U.K. surveys are excluded, the housing elasticities in Houthakker's study range from ·61 to 1·12 and in several cases are not significantly different from 1. A study by Muth (1960), using different methods, also throws doubt upon the validity of Schwabe's law.

Clothing and miscellaneous items, on the other hand, generally show income elasticities above 1 and thus rank as relative luxuries. This is not surprising since the weighted mean of all elasticities is unity, and if some goods have a lower elasticity, others must have a higher elasticity.

Of course, the group of miscellaneous items consists of a hetero-geneous collection of goods and services, the elasticities for which may well be expected to vary a good deal. This in fact is the case in any particular enquiry, but as the results also vary considerably between

97

enquiries, no clear general picture emerges. Some commodity groups present special problems; for example, the amounts spent on alcoholic drink are often under-recorded in a household budget enquiry, and the results are consequently inaccurate. The demand for domestic service depends not only on household income but also on the housewife's working status which in turn influences household income; this should be noted when interpreting the results, as has been pointed out by Mincer (1963) to illustrate a general principle.

The results for individual commodities are generally less accurate than results for commodity groups, as evidenced by relatively large standard errors. This also means that in such a case, the result even for the average income elasticity, to say nothing of its variations over the income range, depends to a large extent on the form of the Engel function chosen. Prais and Houthakker (1971) estimated the income elasticities for six groups of foodstuffs, each based on five alternative forms of regression equations; the range in which the answers lie is given as follows:

Farinaceous foods	·25– ·36
Dairy produce	·35– ·53
Vegetables	·40– ·62
Fruit	·66–1·20
Fish	·51– ·84
Meat	·44– ·69

The variations are substantial. In some enquiries, the data permit a clear-cut answer as to which function gives the best fit for a particular commodity, though even then a compromise may have to be struck, as for the purpose of comparison it is useful to have the same function for all commodities, or least for all commodities of a major group.

In some cases it is also possible to establish the way in which the elasticity varies when total outlay increases. Some fairly complex behaviour, e.g. an increase followed by a decrease in elasticity, may occur. A large number of income groups are necessary to establish such findings.

Of course, income elasticities are not the only things that can be derived from family budget data. An interesting by-product is the effect of family size on expenditure patterns. In (6.7) the coefficient γ_i or its estimate c_i also represent a kind of elasticity which can be interpreted accordingly. Houthakker (1957) found that the coefficients c_i were positive for all budget studies surveyed with regard to food, negative for all studies in the case of miscellaneous items, and mostly negative in the case of housing (results vary for clothing).

This means that with given total outlay, larger households are forced to devote a larger share of the budget to food than smaller households. Consequently they have to economize on items less urgently required, in particular on housing space or quality, in spite of greater " need " for housing; this need cannot be measured.

Some analyses show the differences in expenditure patterns associated with age of children and with social class. Gollnick (1959) analyses 3-person and 4-person households in 1950–51 separately, and in either case assumes additive effects on expenditure. For households of 2 adults and 1 child, 2 dummy variables are introduced to distinguish between children aged 0–5, 6–13 and 14+ years, and 2 dummy variables to distinguish between manual workers, clerical workers and civil servants.

Exercise 6.2　How many dummy variables are required for households of 2 adults and 2 children in the various age-groups? Give a specimen set of dummy variables and indicate what their regression coefficients show.

Gollnick's findings for major commodity groups in 3-person households are higher outlay on food and on beverages and tobacco, together with lower outlay on furniture and furnishings, in households with an older child than in households with a small child. This, of course, reflects not so much the needs of children at different ages as the needs of the household at different periods since the date of marriage. Furthermore, clerical workers spend less than manual workers of the same income level on food, drink and tobacco and more on house rent; this applies even more so to civil servants' households, who also spend more than others on personal hygiene and medical goods and services. Differences observed in other expenditure groups are generally small and not statistically significant.

6.3　Analysis of market data

The influence of prices on quantity or value of a commodity consumed cannot be derived from a single household budget enquiry but generally requires a comparison over time. When budget enquiries are available for different periods they may be utilized for this purpose; otherwise recourse must be had to market data or to statistics of national expenditure. The chief difficulty here is the multiplicity of factors which may have an influence on purchases. The description of demand in the form of a simple relationship between price and quantity of a commodity, corresponding to the notion of the demand curve in economic theory, is not always realistic.

There are, however, some cases in which the study of simple price–quantity relationships seems a legitimate procedure. One condition is that fluctuations in price and quantity must be sufficiently large for their relation to be measurable, whilst variations in income and other disturbing influences should be relatively small. Furthermore there should be little substitution by other products, and the goods should be of limited durability, so that speculative influences and stock holdings have a minimal effect. In addition, there is the practical requirement of adequate data.

It is readily seen that these conditions are in general more nearly satisfied with agricultural commodities than with industrial products. It is therefore no accident that the earlier demand studies were mainly concerned with agricultural products. A very detailed and systematic investigation of the demand for sugar, corn, cotton, hay, wheat, potatoes, oats, barley, rye and buckwheat in the United States was undertaken by Schultz (1938).

In studying the demand for sugar, Schultz uses annual data from 1875 to 1929, but separate functions were derived for three periods. The regressions were not directly fitted to price and quantity but to adjusted variables; the sugar price was divided by a general price index so as to represent the price at 1913 purchasing power, and the quantity was divided by population size. A trend was also allowed for by directly introducing time as a variable or, alternatively, by trend-ratios or link relatives. Furthermore, quantity and price were alternatively used as dependent variables. An index of industrial production was experimentally introduced as a further variable, though it did not significantly improve the fit.

For 1875–95, one of the equations obtained was

$$\log q = 2{\cdot}0559 - {\cdot}3828 \log p + {\cdot}0068t + u$$

where q represents per capita consumption in lb, p the deflated wholesale price in cents per lb, and t time in years ($t = 0$ for 1885). Logarithms to base 10 were used, and the equation could therefore be written as

$$q = 113{\cdot}7\, p^{-{\cdot}3828}\, e^{{\cdot}0156t}\, e^{u}$$

Thus, the estimated price elasticity of demand is $-{\cdot}38$ and consumption per head at unchanged price increases by $1\frac{1}{2}$ per cent per annum. Both results are plausible, as one would imagine the demand for sugar to be inelastic with regard to price and income; the trend increase may reflect an increase with income per head but less than proportionately.

Exercise 6.3 The equation in linear form is

$$q = 70 \cdot 62 - 2 \cdot 259\,p + \cdot 8371 t + u$$

Interpret the result with the help of $\bar{p} = 8 \cdot 319$. What does this form of equation imply regarding changes over time in price elasticity?

Schultz (1938) includes some studies that dig deeper into demand relationships. Realizing the possibilities of substitution between specific commodities, the demand for related foods is studied as a function of not only their own price but also the price of substitutes or complementary goods. The demand for beef, pork and mutton as well as that for barley, corn, hay and oats, and for sugar, tea and coffee, are thus analysed.

With many consumer goods it seems necessary or advisable to introduce a fairly large number of explanatory variables, and to eliminate by empirical study those that are not required. This approach has been followed by Stone (1945) in his relatively early work relating to beer, spirits, tobacco, soap, telegrams, food, consumer durables and motor cars in the United Kingdom 1920–38 and the United States 1929–41. His general model may be written

$$\log q = \alpha + \beta_1 \log Q + \beta_2 \log p + \beta_3 \log \pi + \beta_4\,t + \varepsilon \qquad (6.8)$$

where Q denotes real income and π the price of consumer goods and services other than the commodity or group of goods investigated. To these variables others are added in specific cases.

In the case of U.K. beer consumption, the strength of beer g was added as a further variable, so that five independent variables are available. The regression in the full set and various subsets of variables were investigated with the aid of bunch map analysis. It was then found that if two independent variables are to be chosen, $\log p$ and $\log \pi$ together give the best fit with $R^2 = \cdot 978$. The introduction of g somewhat improves the fit, whilst Q and t are superfluous variables; they could be introduced singly if desired, though the use of the full set of variables is not recommended.

The alternative equations obtained may be written

$$\log q = -1 \cdot 022 \log p + \cdot 947 \log \pi + u$$
$$\log q = - \cdot 939 \log p + \cdot 910 \log \pi + \cdot 363 \log g + u$$
$$\log q = - \cdot 727 \log p + \cdot 914 \log \pi + \cdot 816 \log g + \cdot 136 \log Q + u$$
$$\log q = - \cdot 673 \log p + 1 \cdot 000 \log \pi + 1 \cdot 231 \log g + \cdot 0063 t \log e + u$$

The coefficients are of the expected sign, and the direct price elasticity is obtained as -1 or somewhat lower (in absolute value). It seems, however, paradoxical that real income should have so little effect on beer consumption.

The difficulty with which such an analysis is confronted lies in the high correlations between some of the variables, including particularly time, and the data may not be good enough to allow an accurate isolation of the various effects. To reduce these difficulties, cross-section data and time-series are sometimes used in combination. Thus an income elasticity is estimated from household budgets and substituted into the regression equation to allow a better estimation of price effects. This is basically the method used by Stone (1954a). Of course, the use of cross-section elasticities should not be made mechanically, but often calls for some adjustments and thus for some judgment.

Further strides have been made in demand analysis for agricultural commodities when the full implications of a supply function in operation were realized. The identification problem arising in this context was recognized at an early date, and the possibility of a single-equation estimation bias was noted later on. Where appropriate, both demand and supply relationships should therefore be fully specified before estimation is undertaken. A simple model is of the type

$$q = \alpha_1 + \beta_1 p + \gamma_1 Y + \varepsilon_1$$
$$q = \alpha_2 + \beta_2 p + \gamma_2 z + \varepsilon_2$$

where q indicates quantity produced and sold, p price, Y income or another specific demand factor, and z a specific supply factor indicating climatic conditions or cost. In this case, both equations are exactly identified and may be estimated by indirect least squares.

The equations may, of course, contain additional specific variables; over-identification is then present and with it the need for two-stage least-squares or a similar technique. The model may also contain additional equations. Studies of this kind were made by Girshick and Haavelmo (1947) and by Tintner (1951).

An alternative consists in the specification of time lags which, together with assumptions about the disturbances, make the model recursive. This procedure was followed in the pioneering study by Wold (1959) and other subsequent ones. The basic idea implies treating supply s and demand d as separate variables, measured by production and consumption data respectively. A complete model may then contain a supply function, a demand function and a price-fixing equation which describes an adjustment process in the face of disequilibrium between demand and supply. These equations may and should be estimated separately.

Stojkovicz (1964) formulates an equation system for onions in the

United States, which in terms of the variables defined above may be written as

$$\log s = \alpha_1 + \beta_1 \log p_{-1} + \gamma_1 \log p'_{-1} + \gamma_2 K + \varepsilon_1$$
$$\log d = \alpha_2 + \beta_2 \log p + \gamma_3 \log Y + \varepsilon_2$$
$$\log p = \alpha_3 + \beta_3 (\log d_{-1} - \log s) + \gamma_4 \log Y + \varepsilon_3$$

in which p' is a price index for all vegetables and K a dummy variable which is 1 for war years and 0 otherwise; all quantities and income are *per capita* and time lags refer to one year. It is clearly seen that the causal chain goes from the lagged variables to current supply, then to current price and finally to current demand. This model is compared with an interdependent system without a price equation

$$\log q = \alpha_1 + \beta_1 \log p + \gamma_1 \log p' + \gamma_2 K + \varepsilon_1$$
$$\log q = \alpha_2 + \beta_2 \log p + \gamma_3 \log Y + \varepsilon_2$$

The interdependent model was estimated by two-stage least squares but did not yield acceptable results for the supply elasticities. On the other hand, one version of the recursive model yielded the equations

$$\log s = 1 \cdot 326 + \cdot 179 \log p_{-1} + \cdot 061 \log p'_{-1} + \cdot 022 K + u_1$$
$$\log d = \cdot 901 - \cdot 213 \log p + \cdot 434 \log Y + u_2$$
$$\log p = - \cdot 680 + \cdot 999 (\log d_{-1} - \log s) + \cdot 861 \log Y + u_3$$

and thereby plausible results, for example price elasticities of supply and demand in the neighbourhood of $\cdot 2$ and $- \cdot 2$ respectively. It seems safe to conclude that the recursive specification is superior to the interdependent one in this case. Generally speaking, it seems important to pay attention to correct model specification, which may vary from commodity to commodity in accordance with production and market conditions.

6.4 Complete sets of demand functions

Instead of studying the demand for individual commodities, demand analysis may be concerned with all commodities forming the consumers' budget at the same time. A static picture is obtained from household budgets, but if changes over time and in different price situations are studied, national expenditure data form the main statistical basis. The data then do not refer to individual commodities but to broader or finer commodity groupings.

Even so, the problem may be fairly complex. According to the theory of consumers' demand, quantity or real expenditure on each group depends on total expenditure and on the prices or price indices for each of the groups which are distinguished. Thus with k groups, each regression equation contains $k+1$ regression coefficients to be estimated, apart from the constant term. With any classification that would be of interest the number of parameters to be estimated would be prohibitively large.

It is true that demand theory imposes some restrictions. In the Slutsky equations which are derived from theory and which may be written

$$Eq_j/Ep_i = -w_i Eq_j/EC + w_i \sigma_{ij} \qquad (6.9)$$

σ_{ij} represents the elasticity of substitution between groups i and j if $j \neq i$. It is a fundamental property that

$$\sigma_{ij} = \sigma_{ji} \qquad (6.10)$$

for all pairs of commodity groups. This relation implies some relationship between elasticities of demand, and thus some parameter restrictions in the demand functions, which may be specified, for example, as being linear in the price, quantity and income variables, or as linear in their logarithms. But this still leaves too many constants to be estimated, and further assumptions are necessary.

A system of linear expenditure functions which satisfies the main theoretical conditions is that of Stone (1954b). The idea underlying the model is that expenditure consists of a committed and an uncommitted part; committed expenditure secures a set of basic quantities at existing prices whatever the price level may be, whilst uncommitted expenditure is distributed in fixed proportions over all groups. The main statistical difficulty is the estimation of the basic quantities, which requires an iterative procedure.

In a study for Australia, as also elsewhere, Leser (1960) assumes that with suitable commodity grouping, the cross elasticities of substitution $\sigma_{ij}(j \neq i)$ do not differ much from each other and that the differences may be neglected. A system of linear relations in prices, total outlay and time is set up; in terms of the common value α of the cross substitution elasticities it may be written as

$$v_i = (1-\alpha)\, p_i \bar{q}_i + \alpha \bar{w}_i \sum_{j=1}^{k} p_j \bar{q}_j + \beta_i \left(C - \sum_{j=1}^{k} p_j \bar{q}_j\right) + \gamma_i t + \varepsilon_i$$

$$(i = 1, ..., k) \qquad (6.11)$$

An estimate a is made for α by minimizing a linear combination of residual sums of squares. When a is substituted for α into (6.11), the equations become

$$v_i - (1-a) \, p_i \, \bar{q}_i - a\bar{w}_i \sum_{j=1}^{k} p_j \, \bar{q}_j = \beta_i \, (C - \sum_{j=1}^{k} p_j \, \bar{q}_j) + \gamma_i \, t + \varepsilon_i$$

$$(i = 1, ..., k) \qquad (6.12)$$

Thus the deviations of actual commodity group expenditure from an expected value appear as linear functions of an indicator of real total outlay and of time. Estimates b_i and c_i can then be obtained in the ordinary way.

Using Australian data for 11 financial years from 1949/50 to 1959/60, a compromise between two values minimizing different linear combinations of residual sums yields $a = \cdot 5$, and the estimated average income elasticities are:

Food	·56
Clothing	1·23
Housing	1·16
Gas and Electricity	·24
Durable household goods	1·35
Other goods	·52
Fares	·35
Tobacco and drink	·41
Services	2·08

The time trend shows a substantial shift away from " Clothing " and " Fares " towards " Housing ", " Gas and Electricity " and " Services ". The sensitivity of the results for income elasticities and shifts over time with regard to the assumptions about the substitution elasticities is also examined; by and large, the estimates are fairly robust.

The direct price elasticities obtained for the various groups lie between $-\cdot 76$ and $-\cdot 49$. These results, of course, stand or fall with the assumptions made and, even if these are realistic, with the value of a.

A different assumption is made by Frisch (1959) who introduces the notion of want-independence which is assumed to exist between reasonably aggregated commodity groups. For any good that is want-independent of all other goods, the direct price elasticity is related to the good's income elasticity. It is only necessary to estimate one parameter, interpreted as the money flexibility and the Engel elasticities; the direct price elasticities can then be immediately deduced. Cross price elasticities can also be obtained with the aid of certain assumptions about want-independence.

There are some theoretically questionable features about Frisch's model which assumes measurability of utility; whilst the generally accepted results of demand theory hold with transformations of the utility function, this is not the case here. A theory of neutral want-association which escapes this criticism has been developed and applied to econometric studies by Pearce (1964). For goods in neutral want-association with all others, it implies that the cross elasticities of substitution are proportionate to the income elasticities of both goods concerned, and the direct elasticities of substitution approximately proportionate to the income elasticities.

Applying the theory to 15 commodity groups for the United Kingdom in 1957, Pearce obtains the following income and direct price elasticities:

	Eq_i/EY	Eq_i/Ep_i
Food	1·34	−1·13
Alcohol, tobacco	·36	− ·37
Housing, fuel	·58	− ·57
Household durables	1·56	−1·41
Other household	·63	− ·59
Clothing	·96	− ·90
Books, newspapers, etc.	·44	− ·41
Other recreational	·69	− ·64
Chemists' goods	·79	− ·74
Other miscellaneous goods	·71	− ·67
Motoring, travel	2·29	−1·92
Communication	1·00	− ·93
Entertainment	·22	− ·20
Domestic services	0	0
Other services	·30	− ·29

Powell (1966) uses similar assumptions to obtain revised estimates of income and price elasticities for Australia. Data revisions and use of longer time series substantially raise the estimated income elasticities for durable household goods and for other goods above the levels obtained in Leser's study; the income elasticity for services is much reduced, and an income elasticity of 2·50 for motor vehicles and running expenses is also obtained. The new method affects the values of the income elasticities only marginally, but the direct price elasticities now range from − ·14 for gas and electricity to −1·05 for motor vehicles and running expenses.

It is a consequence of the assumptions made and the method used in these two studies that numerically high price elasticities are obtained for expenditure items with high income elasticity, and numerically low price elasticities for items with low income elasticity. This is on the whole plausible with broad commodity groups, but the differences might not be as large as indicated here.

106

A modified theoretical scheme lies at the heart of the method developed by Barten (1964) and applied to 14 commodity groups covering about 70 per cent of all consumers' expenditure, " rent " and other commodities and services being excluded for practical reasons, for the Netherlands over the periods 1921–39 and 1948–58. A system of linear functions in the logarithms of prices, total outlay and quantities is formulated, using first differences throughout the analysis and assuming interactions to be non-zero for 11 pairs of commodities only. The resulting system of equations with parameter restrictions is subjected to several rounds of estimation, prior information about elasticities from other sources being incorporated in the final estimates.

The final estimates of income and direct price elasticities range from ·12 and −·05 respectively for bread to 1·49 and −·89 respectively for durables other than household articles, the signs of the estimates for bread from the data being changed by the use of prior information. The cross price elasticities, with the exception of those between groceries and dairy products, do not differ significantly from 0; therefore there is little evidence for specific substitution effects.

6.5 Dynamic demand functions

In all the demand studies considered hitherto, demand is considered as dependent on the current level of economic variables, without taking into account past experience or future expectations and plans. Even though a time trend may be introduced, such demand functions are essentially static ones. A change in one or more explanatory variables is envisaged as bringing about immediately a movement from one equilibrium, or optimum position, to another.

In a dynamic analysis the influence of a change in a variable is carried on after its immediate effect. It follows that a distinction must be made between short-run and long-run effects; and the econometric problem now includes the estimation of short-term and long-term demand elasticities.

The dynamic element may be introduced into the model through lagged variables which are brought explicitly into the demand equations. The time-lag need not be fixed but may be distributed over a long period. The use of distributed lags in demand analysis with its difficulties and potentialities has been discussed particularly by Nerlove (1958).

The need for model building of this kind becomes particularly acute in the context of durable goods, purchases of which may be viewed as adjustments to a desired level of stocks in the hands of the public. It follows that actual stocks become an important explanatory variable. Early studies in this field refer to dwelling units and motor cars, for both of which stock data are available from published sources. Pioneer studies were made, among others, by Derksen (1940) for new housing and by Roos and von Szeliski (1939) for motor cars.

Chow (1957) starts a systematic investigation by relating the *per capita* stock X of motor cars in the United States to a relative price index p and either to an indicator of *per capita* income I or to an estimate of the money stock per head M. The use of I follows from existing demand theory, and the use of M from an alternative theory by which holdings of consumer durables are in constant proportion to money holdings. Expected income per head I_e, derived from current and past incomes, is found to be a better indicator in this equation than disposable income per head I_d. Two estimates of money stock are also used, one of them being total money stock per head M_a.

Data for the 33 years from 1921 to 1953 are used and price is chosen as the dependent variable in the regressions, but afterwards the equations are rearranged to facilitate interpretation. Two alternative equations obtained are:

$$\log X = -6\cdot28 - \cdot95 \log p + 2\cdot03 \log I_e + u$$

or $\qquad \log X = -\cdot26 - 1\cdot46 \log p + 1\cdot57 \log M_a + u$

Both equations give a good fit. The price elasticity for the stock of motor cars is thus estimated at about -1 or $-1\cdot5$, and there is either an income elasticity of about 2 or a money stock elasticity of about $1\cdot5$.

From thereon, Chow proceeds to construct functions explaining new purchases of cars, again testing various theories. One function giving a good explanation relates new purchases to car price, stock at the beginning of the year, and disposable income; it represents a dynamic demand function combined with a savings function.

The difficulty of getting data for stocks of consumer durables led investigators to search for models which do not explicitly include stocks among the variables or in which stocks can be estimated from other data. Such a model, in which consumption and stocks were estimated by means of assumed depreciation rates for stock and new purchases, was constructed by Stone and Rowe (1958). Consumption q' in this model depends on opening stock s and on the desired equilibrium stock level s^* which in turn depends on real income or expenditure C, relative price p, and time t. The equations may be formulated as

$$q' = \alpha'_1 \, s^{*\rho} \, s^{1-\rho}$$
$$s^* = \alpha'_2 \, C^\beta \, p^\gamma \, e^{\delta t}$$

Thus $\qquad q' = \alpha' \, C^{\beta\rho} \, p^{\gamma\rho} \, e^{\delta\rho t} \, s^{1-\rho}$ $\qquad\qquad$ (6.13)

When applying least squares to the regression of $\log q'$ on the logarithms of the other variables, the function becomes

$$(\log q')_c = a + br \log C + cr \log p + drt + (1-r) \log s \qquad (6.14)$$

The model is applicable to perishable goods, for which s is replaced by lagged consumption q'_{-1}. The coefficients br and cr represent estimates of short-term elasticities of consumption with regard to income and price. The parameter r estimates the adjustment rate, i.e. the proportion by which the difference between actual and desired stocks (in logarithms) is reduced within one period. The short-term elasticities of purchases near equilibrium are brm and crm, where m is the length of life for new equipment. The long-term elasticities of consumption or purchases are given by b and c which are derived from br, cr and $1-r$.

In this study, 10 commodity groups were analysed. Quarterly data for consumers' expenditure in the United Kingdom from 1950 to 1956 are used in the form of first differences and of deviations from quarterly means. Temperature and rainfall are introduced as additional variables and are retained wherever the regression coefficient is significant. Also real total expenditure lagged one quarter is used, together with the current total, and the values of br given below are the sums of two regression coefficients. The results obtained were as follows:

Group	br	cr	$1-r$
Beer	·68	− ·53	− ·31
Other alcoholic drink	3·23	1·52	− ·47
Tobacco	1·00	− ·78	− ·20
Fuel and light	− ·06	− ·66	− ·10
Durable household goods	·20	− ·014	·91
Furniture	·21	− ·012	·88
Hardware	·12	− ·06	·95
Footwear	·49	− ·08	·69
Other clothing	·44	− ·09	·73
Entertainment	·42	− ·33	− ·29

r is seen to be small for the household durables, somewhat larger for clothing but greater than 1 for the perishable goods analysed here. This means that adjustment is slow for the household goods, but that there is over-adjustment in any one period for the perishable goods.

The low short-term elasticities for the durable goods only refer to consumption. To derive approximate elasticities for purchases the figures for clothing have to be multiplied by 5·7 and those for household goods by 28·2. Fairly high values for elasticities are then obtained.

Stone and Rowe also compute the long-term elasticities and compare the figures with results derived from time-series 1920–37 and budget data 1937–39. In some cases, combined estimates are made; since the present estimates generally have relatively high standard errors, their weight in the combined estimates is generally low.

Exercise 6.4 Compute estimates of the long-term income and price elasticities b and c. Which results seem doubtful?

The study quoted is only one in a series by the authors. In a later study by Stone and Rowe (1960) the depreciation rates are not assumed *a priori* but are estimated themselves from the data. This involves linearizing the equations in the original variables and applying a transformation in such a way that the depreciation rates may be derived from the partial regression coefficients in the transformed equations.

A different approach again is followed by Cramer (1962) who studies ownership rather than purchases or consumption of durable goods. Cross-section data are used to estimate the effect of income, net worth and other variables on ownership. The main results for aggregate elasticities of ownership obtained under certain assumptions are:

Commodity	Income elasticity	Net worth elasticity
Refrigerators	·96	·93
Washing machines	·74	·54
Motor cars	·69	·86
Television sets	·30	·33

The sum of these elasticities may be interpreted as a long-term income elasticity, in contrast to the short-term elasticity given.

Houthakker and Taylor (1966) also consider the effect of stocks upon demand but manage to eliminate stocks entirely from the demand equations. Their basic model, in which q indicates quantity bought, s stocks, Y income, also $\dot{q}$, $\dot{S}$ and $\dot{Y}$ derivatives with regard to time, is as follows:

$$q = \alpha + \beta S + \gamma Y$$
$$\dot{S} = q - \delta S$$

the second equation assuming a constant depreciation rate. With the help of the derived equation

$$\dot{q} = \beta \dot{S} + \gamma \dot{Y}$$

the demand equation reduces to the form

$$\dot{q} = \alpha\delta + (\beta - \delta)q + \gamma\dot{Y} + \gamma\delta Y$$

Estimates of the parameters α, β, γ and δ may therefore be derived from the coefficients in a regression of $\dot{q}$ on q, $\dot{Y}$ and Y. In practice, a discrete approximation is made which permits the use of a regression of q on q_{-1}, Y and Y_{-1}.

Prices may also be introduced into the demand function, though this implies over-identification and the use of an iterative procedure. Furthermore, the method is extended to perishable goods, in the case of which S is interpreted as psychological stock. A negative value of β indicates adjustment to desired stock level; a positive value indicates habit formation, that is to say, a positive effect of past on current purchases.

The method, with various refinements, is applied to 84 categories of personal consumption expenditure in the United States, to derive demand functions and projections into the future. A striking result is the predominance of habit formation over stock adjustment.

Instead of introducing actual or psychological stocks of a commodity into the demand function for that commodity, Leser (1971b) uses stocks of durable goods, which are estimated from the data with the help of regression, as an explanatory variable for all commodity groups distinguished in the analysis; this replaces the use of a time trend and is felt to be more satisfactory. The method is applied to United Kingdom national accounts data for 13 commodity groups over the period 1950–67 and yields, among other things, estimates of both short run and long run income elasticities of demand. For motoring, for example, the short run income elasticity is 1·0 but the long run elasticity 4·2; the difference is accounted for by the purchase of motor cars in response to higher income and a subsequent change of expenditure pattern.

All in all, demand analysis has branched out in various directions, with a general tendency towards more sophisticated model specification. Advanced estimation techniques are also used, but relatively simple estimation methods have their place too. The practical importance of demand forecasting is obvious, and econometric analysis can make a valuable contribution in this field.

6.1

$$w_{ic} = a_i + b_i \log C$$

$$v_{ic} = a_i C + b_i C \log C$$

$$(\partial v_i / \partial C)_c = a_i + b_i (1 + \log C)$$

$$= w_{ic} + b_i$$

$$(Ev_i / EC)_c = 1 + b_i / w_{ic}$$

$$\overline{Ev_i} / EC = 1 + b_i / \overline{w}_i$$

$b_i > 0$ indicates elastic, $b_i < 0$ inelastic demand.

6.2 Five dummy variables are required. They could be chosen as follows:

Children's age groups	d_1	d_2	d_3	d_4	d_5
0–5, 0–5	0	0	0	0	0
0–5, 6–13	1	0	0	0	0
0–5, 14+	0	1	0	0	0
6–13, 6–13	0	0	1	0	0
6–13, 14+	0	0	0	1	0
14+, 14+	0	0	0	0	1

The coefficients then show the contrast between households with small children and households with one or both children in the higher age groups.

6.3

$$\bar{q} = 70 \cdot 62 - 2 \cdot 259 \times 8 \cdot 319 + 0$$

$$= 51 \cdot 83$$

$$\overline{Eq} / Ep = -2 \cdot 259 \times 8 \cdot 319 / 51 \cdot 83$$

$$= - \cdot 36$$

$$(\partial q / \partial t) / \bar{q} = \cdot 8371 / 51 \cdot 83$$

$$= \cdot 016$$

An increase in price by 1 cent reduces consumption by more than 2 lb per head. On the average, this implies a price elasticity of $-\cdot 36$. Consumption per head tends to increase by almost 1 lb per annum, or at the average consumption level of 52 lb by 1·6 per cent. The assumptions imply a decrease in price elasticity over time.

6.4

	b	c
Beer	·52	− ·40
Other alcoholic drink	2·20	1·03
Tobacco	·83	− ·65
Fuel and light	− ·05	− ·60
Durable household goods	2·22	− ·16
Furniture	1·75	− ·10
Hardware	2·40	−1·20
Footwear	1·58	− ·26
Other clothing	1·63	− ·33
Entertainment	·33	− ·26

(Some rounding errors; more accurate figures given by Stone and Rowe.) b seems too high for " other alcoholic drink ", " hardware " and " footwear ", too low for " fuel " and " entertainment ". c has an improbable positive value for " other alcoholic drink ", and $|c|$ seems too high for " fuel and light " and " hardware ", too low for " durable household goods ", " furniture " and " entertainment ".

7. MACRO-ECONOMIC MODELS

7.1 The consumption function

It has been seen that in many econometric applications, e.g. demand studies for individual commodities, a single equation approach is acceptable, as any possible repercussions which the dependent variable may have on the independent variables are very indirect or negligible. This does not apply when dealing with macro-economic totals like national income, consumption, investment or imports; and in studying relations between these a simultaneous equation approach is usually called for. Even if the model is such that a single equation estimation is appropriate, this should be explicitly established and noted.

An important example of a macro-economic relation is the consumption function which in its simplest form may be written as

$$C = \alpha + \beta Y \tag{7.1}$$

where C is total consumption expenditure, often including current government expenditure together with personal outlay, and Y an indicator of income which may be gross national product, national income, or disposable income; the variables may be measured in value or real terms. In (7.1), β represents the marginal propensity to consume, and $1/(1-\beta)$ the multiplier, both of those being concepts which have attracted a great deal of interest in economic theory following the work of Keynes. Efforts were therefore made by various investigators to establish numerical values for β or $1/(1-\beta)$.

A systematic study of the problem was made by Stone and Stone (1938). Besides other methods, regression analysis was applied to time-series for Germany, Great Britain, the Netherlands, Poland, Sweden and the United States. In some cases, different regressions were estimated for different periods. Time was used as additional variable and was retained or dropped from the final equation as appropriate. The resulting estimates of the marginal propensity to consume varied between ·423 for Germany in 1932–36 and ·795 for Sweden in 1896–1916. The corresponding multipliers varied between 1·7 and 4·9.

The simple formulation (7.1) has been criticized on several grounds. Haavelmo (1947) pointed out that even assuming (7.1) to be realistic it should be read in conjunction with the identity

$$Y = C + Z \tag{7.2}$$

where Z represents investment in the form of both fixed capital formation and stock increases, plus the excess of exports over imports (which may be negative). Z is considered to be an exogenous variable whilst Y and C are endogenous. Combination of (7.1) and (7.2) yields the reduced form

$$Y = \alpha/(1-\beta)+Z/(1-\beta) \atop C = \alpha/(1-\beta)+\beta Z/(1-\beta) \Bigg\} \qquad (7.3)$$

To obtain consistent estimates least squares should be applied to (7.3) to obtain in the first place an estimate of $1/(1-b)$ or $b/(1-b)$. Application of least squares to (7.1) leads to inconsistent estimates.

From United States data for 1922–41 Haavelmo obtained the estimate

$$1/(1-b_{\text{RF}}) = 3 \cdot 05$$

with 95 per cent confidence limits 2·33 and 3·76. Direct least squares yielded

$$b_{\text{SE}} = \cdot 732$$

Exercise 7.1 Compare the two estimates and comment.

Other econometric studies contain more complex consumption functions based on various theories. In some cases, lagged terms in Y or C or both are introduced, following the idea that changes in income do not all take effect immediately but some time elapses before consumption plans are adjusted. Alternatively, the influence of wealth may be stressed, and a term with liquid asset holdings is introduced. Again, following Duesenberry (1949) and Modigliani (1949) the highest level of income ever obtained may retain its influence through the formation of habits.

Klein (1950) constructed two simple models and one more elaborate model for the United States. Model II consists of a consumption function and an identity

$$C/pN = \alpha+\beta_1 Y/pN+\beta_2 (Y/pN)_{-1}+\beta_3 (M/pN)_{-1}+\varepsilon \atop Y+T = C+I+G \Bigg\} \quad (7.4)$$

where C indicates consumption, Y disposable income, M money supply, T net taxes, I gross investment, and G government expenditure and foreign balances, all in current prices; p is a cost-of-living index and N population size. The equations were converted into reduced form and the parameters estimated from annual data for 1922–41. The resulting equation was

$$Y/pN = 186 \cdot 53+ \cdot 30(Y/pN)_{-1}+ \cdot 13(M/pN)_{-1}+2 \cdot 36\ (I+G-T)/pN+u,$$

but the coefficient of $(M/pN)_{-1}$ was found to be non-significant and a fit which was almost as good was given by the equation

$$Y/pN = 202 \cdot 54+ \cdot 37(Y/pN)_{-1}+2 \cdot 39\ (I+G-T)/pN+u$$

Thus the influence of lagged disposable income seems established, but the influence of money holdings is not.

Exercise 7.2   From the last equation, show that the coefficients of Y/pN and $(Y/pN)_{-1}$ in the structural equation for C/pN add up to about ·74, and interpret the result.

A different result was obtained by Zellner (1957) who used quarterly data, seasonally adjusted, for the U.S. from 1947 to 1955 (first quarter). The main variables, all measured at constant prices, are personal consumption C, personal disposable income Y, and liquid assets at the beginning of the quarter L_{-1}, together with lagged values of C and Y and with their past peak values indicated by ^{0}. Ten consumption functions with different variable specifications were fitted by ordinary least squares, two of them also by the reduced-form method. A function was then considered acceptable if the coefficient signs were economically meaningful, the coefficients were significant, and the residuals non-autocorrelated. Out of the functions estimated by ordinary least squares, two were thus considered acceptable and a further one provisionally acceptable as the Durbin–Watson test was inconclusive. These functions were:

Function	R^2_{adj}	d
$C = -21{\cdot}9 + {\cdot}708\ Y + {\cdot}368\ L_{-1}$	·979	1·79
$C = -19{\cdot}0 + {\cdot}375\ Y + {\cdot}219\ L_{-1} + {\cdot}489\ C_{-1}$	·984	1·77
$C = -23{\cdot}0 + {\cdot}458\ Y + {\cdot}272\ L_{-1} + {\cdot}369\ C^0$	·982	1·54

The hypothesis that the level of liquid assets, together with disposable income, largely determines the level of consumption thus appears to be confirmed by the data. The influence of previous consumption levels appears more doubtful; and there is little guidance as to the exact way in which they enter the consumption function.

This illustrates one of the difficulties encountered in econometric research. It is often possible to obtain a good fit by various combinations of variables, and it is difficult to decide which one to choose. This applies particularly in macro-economic analysis where the theoretical relations are not often firmly established.

Subsequent work on the consumption function has been influenced by the formulation of the permanent income hypothesis and the suggestions for estimating permanent income and permanent consumption made by Friedman (1957), as well as a trend towards disaggregation, distinguishing particularly between expenditure on durable goods and other consumer expenditure. The boundary between macro-economic relationships and demand analysis is thereby becoming blurred. A study by Zellner, Huang and Chau (1965) indicates the direction of further research.

7.2 Model-building problems

With the help of a consumption function, the level of national consumption expenditure may be predicted from an assumed or estimated level of gross national product or investment. In practice, it is often desired to derive at the same time the level of other macro-economic variables with the help of further relationships. The consumption function then appears as part of a system of structural equations which constitute an econometric macro-model. In the construction of such a model, various problems arise, and the character of the model depends on the decisions made at various stages of model construction.

Notionally at any rate, the first task is to fix the number of equations in the model by specifying the variables which are to be treated as endogenous. In practice, this need not be done at once; one may start with a limited number of equations and endogenous variables, and may subsequently enlarge the model. The ultimate size of the model then depends on decisions regarding both coverage and degree of disaggregation. Most models contain, as endogenous variables, national accounts entities such as consumption and investment in money terms or real terms, but in addition there may be endogenous variables referring to the labour force, the money market, the field of prices, etc. Furthermore, to give an example, investment may be indicated by a single variable or broken up into residential and other construction, new machinery, stock changes, etc.

The structural equations are most easily interpreted if each equation corresponds clearly to each one of the endogenous variables, which may be written on the left-hand side of the equation; this is not necessarily the case, though. Some equations are behavioural and contain parameters to be estimated; there may be others in the model, for example tax receipts equations, which contain numerical values inserted on the basis of prior considerations. Models normally also contain one or more definitional identities; for example gross domestic or gross national product Y may be defined by the equation

$$Y = C + G + I + S + X - M$$

117

where C indicates personal consumption, G government consumption, I fixed investment, S stockbuilding, X exports, M imports; the equation may appear in a more aggregated or in a more disaggregated form.

In this context it is necessary to decide which of the variables appearing in the identities are endogenous and which are exogenous. Government expenditure for example, is commonly treated as exogenous, as it is considered to be determined by policy considerations. If, however, the level of government expenditure depends upon government receipts which are largely outside government control, then it becomes an endogenous variable.

As the equations are being formulated, additional exogenous and lagged endogenous variables are introduced. Alternative formulations, involving different choices of predetermined variables, may well be made and tried out at a later stage.

The length of the time period to which the flow variables refer is of crucial importance here. Most macro-models use annual or quarterly data. Models using quarterly data obviously have the edge on annual ones from the economic forecasting point of view, since movements of explanatory variables during the year are of importance even for the prediction of annual figures. Quarterly models permit much greater flexibility in the specification of time lags, as one does not have to choose between simultaneity and a year's lag; therefore quarterly models are of a different character from annual ones.

At the same time, the use of quarterly data in a model presents additional problems. Seasonality must be taken care of by dummy variables or by seasonal adjustments; the former may be preferable on grounds of statistical theory, but if seasonally adjusted data are available, they are commonly used for practical reasons. Some variables which one may want to include but for which quarterly data are not available may have to be replaced by proxy variables. Quarterly data are also even more liable to revision than annual ones.

The question whether or not to subject the economic variables to a transformation may come up next. A transformation to logarithms would linearize the multiplicative relationships between prices, quantities and values, but since the most important identities are additive, the application of this device would seldom be advantageous. On the other hand, a transformation to first differences is often made. An important consideration is the fact that the main interest often lies in year-to-year or quarter-to-quarter changes rather than absolute levels, and a good fit in first differences, not only in actual values, is really required. In some models, percentage differences are used instead of absolute differences.

118

When the model has been fully specified, the burdensome task of data collection arises. This may involve a choice between alternative series and troublesome adjustment and reconciliation where there has been a break in the published series.

Estimation of the structural parameters may then be undertaken. Single-equation least squares is frequently used for provisional estimates. The individual equations may then be tested for goodness of fit and the absence of error autocorrelation. If any equation is not considered satisfactory, it may then be modified. In cases where alternative versions of an equation are considered, the preferred version should be selected for retention.

A simultaneous equation estimation method is then chosen where appropriate and applied to obtain final parameter estimates. Generally the reduced-form equations are involved in the estimation. This may lead to difficulties when there is a large number of predetermined variables, exceeding the number of observations. In such a case, the most important predetermined variables, or some of their principal components, may be utilized. For a description of principal component analysis, see for example Kendall (1961).

The model is then ready for application. The model builder must, however, be prepared for disappointing results when using it in connection with data outside the observation period. Further modifications and revisions of the model may therefore be indicated from time to time.

7.3 Some simple models

Econometric macro-models differ from each other in complexity in various ways. The models which are simplest to handle are those containing but a few endogenous variables and thus only a few equations, which moreover are linear functions of other variables and which permit estimation by single-equation or indirect least-squares methods. The violation of these conditions introduces complications which, however, it may be well worthwhile to accept. In view of the complexity of actual economic life, the limitations of small-scale models must be obvious; nevertheless they may fulfil some useful functions.

A very simple quarterly model for the United States was given by Gallaway and Smith (1961). It consists of an identity and three structural equations which are a consumption function, an investment function, and a government expenditure function. These may be written as

$$Y = C+I+G$$
$$C = \alpha_1+\gamma_1 Yd_{-1}+\gamma_2 M+\varepsilon_1$$
$$I = \alpha_2+\gamma_3 (Y_{-1}-Y_{-2})+\gamma_4 Z_{-1}+\varepsilon_2$$
$$G = \alpha_3+\gamma_5 G_{-1}+\varepsilon_3$$

$$(7.5)$$

where Y represents gross national product, C personal consumption, I gross private domestic investment, G government expenditure plus net foreign investment, Yd disposable income, M money supply at the beginning of the quarter, and Z property income before tax. All variables are first differences in current prices, and all lags refer to quarters; M could therefore well have been written as $M_{-1/2}$.

The right-hand side of the structural equations contains only predetermined variables, hence single-equation estimation is applicable. Using seasonally adjusted data for each quarter from 1948 to 1957, the estimated relations are:

$$C = \cdot 09 + \cdot 43 \ Yd_{-1} + \cdot 23 \ M + u_1 \qquad (R^2 = \cdot 23)$$

$$I = \cdot 08 + \cdot 43 \ (Y_{-1} - Y_{-2}) + \cdot 48 \ Z_{-1} + u_2 \qquad (R^2 = \cdot 40)$$

$$G = \cdot 13 + \cdot 67 \ G_{-1} + u_3 \qquad (R^2 = \cdot 42)$$

The coefficient of M is not, and the coefficient of Z_{-1} is barely significant; nevertheless it is not unreasonable to retain these variables in the equations.

The fit of the equations to the data is not very good, even when allowance has been made for the use of first differences, which considerably reduces the value of R^2 compared with regressions based on original data. However, this is not really surprising in view of the fact that the model attempts to explain current changes entirely in terms of the past, without introducing any current explanatory variables.

There are other obvious limitations to the model, for example the absence of any equations for price and volume changes separately. Within the limits of what the model sets out to do it does this in a straightforward manner. It is shown that the model at any rate forecasts the direction of changes quite well, particularly for the gross national product which is obtained by adding the estimated values of the three components.

A mathematical model which has been used in the same form for each of eleven O.E.E.C. member countries has been given by von Hohenbalken and Tintner (1962). It may be written as

120

$$\left.\begin{array}{rcl} C/NP &=& \alpha_1 + \beta_1 \, Y/NP \\ \log X &=& \alpha_2 + \beta_2 \log D \\ dX/dD &=& W/P \\ Y &=& C+K \\ X &=& Y/P \end{array}\right\} \qquad (7.6)$$

The endogenous variables are: C, value of personal consumption; Y, X and P, gross national product in current and constant prices respectively, together with the implied price index; D, total employment. N represents population, W average yearly money earnings per worker, and K public consumption plus investment plus exports minus imports; these variables are treated as exogenous.

There are thus only two behaviour equations in the system, which are a consumption function and a production function. The remaining equations are a labour demand function set up on *a priori* grounds, and two national accounts identities.

The parameters in the consumption function were estimated by indirect least squares with the help of the first of the national accounts identities. The parameters in the production function were also estimated by a combination of the equation with the labour demand function.

Apart from the complication introduced by the variables occurring in both linear and non-linear form and by non-linear identities, the system is basically simple. In some ways it represents an ambitious attempt to assess the effect of changes in various exogenous variables on gross national product, personal consumption, employment, and price changes. Its limitations are shown up, for example, by the result that for all the countries investigated, a rise in earnings, other things being equal, implies a fall in employment and in real gross national product, though a rise in the other endogenous variables.

A model which introduces somewhat complex relationships but does not present any serious estimation problems is that designed by Duesenberry, Eckstein and Fromm (1960) for the special purpose of studying a recession in the United States. The more detailed full model is summarized in four equations, the left-hand side variables being changes in volume of inventories, value of personal income, value of personal disposable income and the ratio of real personal consumption per head to lagged real disposable income per head respectively. The right-hand side variables are mostly exogenous or lagged terms, except that personal income is an explanatory variable in the equation for personal disposable income. The system is thus fully recursive, and the equations may be estimated individually.

The inventory and personal income functions contain, respectively,

121

six and seven explanatory variables, some of them being differences between economic aggregates. Direct estimation of such a large number of parameters would have been of doubtful value; but in fact, the equations have been aggregated from a number of functions for components of inventories or personal income with different explanatory variables. Personal disposable income is obtained as a quadratic function of personal income. The consumption function is based entirely on values lagged one or two quarters and on past peak values. With the help of quarterly data for 1930–38 and 1948–57, the estimated consumption function becomes

$$c/y_{-1} = \cdot535 - \cdot137\, y_{-1}/y^0_{-1} + \cdot570\, c_{-1}/y_{-2}$$

where c is deflated consumption per head, y deflated disposable income per head, ^{0} denotes a past peak value, and the lags are in quarters.

Although the statistical estimation of the equations did not present any methodological difficulties, it does not follow that the construction of the model was an easy matter. For some of the equations or sub-equations a number of alternative formulations had to be examined before a satisfactory result was obtained. Even so, there remains some doubt, e.g. in the consumption function on account of coefficient instability when the full observation period is broken down.

A model which is formulated in simple terms and is almost but not fully recursive has been constructed by Menges (1959) for Western Germany. It consists of an income determination function, an investment function, a consumption function and a profit determination function and may be written as

$$
\left.
\begin{aligned}
Y &= \alpha_1 + \beta_1\, I + \gamma_1\, Y_{-1} + \varepsilon_1 \\
I &= \alpha_2 + \beta_2 Y + \beta_3\, Q + \varepsilon_2 \\
C &= \alpha_3 + \beta_4 Y + \gamma_2\, C_{-1} + \gamma_3\, P + \varepsilon_3 \\
Q &= \alpha_4 + \gamma_4\, Q_{-1} + \gamma_5\, R + \varepsilon_4
\end{aligned}
\right\}
\qquad (7.7)
$$

The endogenous variables are: Y national income, I net capital formation, C personal consumption, and Q profits, all at market prices. Exogenous variables are the cost of living index P and the index of industrial productivity R.

Examination of the system shows that in the fourth equation, Q depends on predetermined variables alone; the equation may therefore be estimated by itself. In the third equation, C depends on Y only, apart from predetermined variables; single-equation estimation is again permissible. Only Y and I, in the first two equations, are well and truly interrelated, and these equations present simultaneous equation problems. The system can be said to be divided into three blocks formed by the equation for Q, those for Y and I, and that for C

respectively; and it can be considered as recursive between the blocks.

Exercise 7.3 Show that the equations for Y and I are identified, and also that they are over-identified.

Annual data from 1950 to 1957 were used for estimation, with 1949 data for lagged terms. The method of full maximum likelihood was applied to the first two equations, and the resulting non-linear equations were solved by iteration, starting from ordinary least-squares parameter estimates.

A comparison of initial (single-equation) and final (maximum likelihood) estimates for the main parameters shows the following picture:

	Initial	Final
b_1	1·391	1·453
c_1	·729	·717
b_2	·027	−·123
b_3	·701	1·293

Thus the parameters in the income determination function seem fairly robust, but those in the investment function rather sensitive to differences in estimation procedure. The full system is

$$\left.\begin{aligned}
Y &= 18\cdot50 + 1\cdot453\,I + \cdot717\,Y_{-1} + u_1 \\
I &= -18\cdot92 - \cdot123\,Y + 1\cdot293\,Q + u_2 \\
C &= 32\cdot98 + \cdot540\,Y + \cdot157\,C_{-1} - \cdot272\,P + u_3 \\
Q &= -13\cdot98 + \cdot145\,Q_{-1} + \cdot425\,R + u_4
\end{aligned}\right\} \quad (7.8)$$

The signs of the coefficients are generally plausible except for the coefficient of Y in the investment function. This is in fact the equation in which erratic coefficients were discovered, and examination of the data shows that multicollinearity is present and accurate estimation is impossible.

7.4 Some properties of larger models

Most econometric models designed for practical application rather than methodological illustration contain from 10 behaviour equations upwards, so as to be able to explain the movements in all those variables which are of chief interest. In addition, some models contain identities, or equations with numerical coefficients which are not estimated but inserted on the basis of *a priori* considerations, or both; the latter type of equation is frequently of the type of a tax transfer, with known taxation rates as coefficients. The number of endogenous variables is then equal to the total number of equations.

The number of exogenous variables introduced is generally of a similar order of magnitude to the number of current endogenous variables; lagged endogenous variables are, of course, also used extensively. With so many variables being available, an identification problem rarely arises in practice, since in the formulation of each equation it seems natural to include only essential variables. Thus sufficient variables—and sufficiently different sets in each equation—are generally excluded to secure identification.

For the same reason, over-identification is the rule rather than the exception. Moreover, macro-economic relationships do not lend themselves as readily to causal specification as demand and supply micro-relationships seem to do, and very few models are of a fully recursive type. Simultaneous equation estimation methods therefore are, or ought to be, employed in most cases.

The pioneering attempt to describe the working of an economy by means of an econometric model was made by Tinbergen (1939) for the United States. The model is a fairly large one, even by present-day standards, as it contains 32 structural equations and 18 identities. Some of the macro-variables are disaggregated; there are, for example, three consumption functions and three investment functions. The monetary sector of the economy is also extensively treated.

At that time, the estimation problems brought on by interdependence of relationships had not been fully realized, and Tinbergen used simple least-squares estimation. Apart from this, the model contains many features which are characteristic of more recent models, such as the use of time-lags and other ways of introducing a dynamic element into the system. The device of linearizing by means of approximation, applied to basically non-linear relations such as exist between price, quantity, and value changes, is also one for which model-makers are indebted to Tinbergen.

Subsequently, econometric model-building was largely developed in the United States under the auspices of the Cowles Commission. Since attention was initially concentrated on methodological studies, the models built were for some time invariably smaller than that of Tinbergen. The relative abundance of adequate statistical series in the United States facilitated the construction of models for that country. A large part of the credit for the work must be given to Klein and his associates. Klein (1950) gave the first sizeable model for the United States built by this school, consisting of 12 structural equations and 4 definitions, using inter-war data as a basis.

The United States model which has perhaps attracted the most attention and which has, until superseded by more recent developments, been extensively used for forecasting, is that of Klein and Goldberger (1955). This represents an attempt to explain the movements in 20 endogenous variables. Of these, 10 are national income and expenditure flow variables in real terms, 4 are deflated stock variables, 3 are price index numbers including a wage rate index, 2 represent security yields, and 1 the number of wage and salary earners. These variables are connected by 5 identities, leaving 15 equations for estimation. In the case of three equations, single-equation estimation was applicable; the remaining 12 were estimated by the limited information method.

Econometric macro-models have been constructed for a number of other countries. A relatively simple model is that for India given by Narasimham (1956). It contains 18 endogenous and 12 exogenous variables, mostly aggregates in current prices and price indices. There are 7 definitional relations, so that 11 variables are to be explained by behaviour relations. These equations refer to: consumption, investment, import and labour demand; price of consumer goods, of capital goods, of farm products, and of labour; corporate and non-corporate profits; and non-corporate income tax. The expressions appearing in the equations are almost all economic variables themselves or linear combinations of economic variables, some of them with time-lags; the exception is a ratio of endogenous employment to exogenous population. Single-equation estimation is employed, and three or fewer partial regression coefficients only had to be estimated for any one equation.

In the Netherlands, the use of econometric models for economic planning found early acceptance, following Tinbergen's work. The model described by the Central Planning Bureau (1961) constitutes a substantially revised version of an earlier model dating from 1955. Like Narasimham's model, it contains 11 reaction equations, of which 7 explain respectively changes in consumption, fixed investment, stock building, exports, imports, employment and unemployment, whilst 4 are price formation equations. Unlike the Indian model, however, it uses a very large number of variables altogether, connected by various definitional relationships. Furthermore, the numerous terms in the equations are in many cases complicated expressions obtained by combination and transformation of economic variables. For example, the indicator used for available labour is not the unemployment percentage itself but a mathematical function of this percentage. The main variables are year-to-year percentage differences. Estimates based on data for 1923–38 and 1949–57 were made by two-stage least squares.

The models referred to so far use annual data. More recently the tendency has been to make use of quarterly data, so as to be able to analyse short-term movements of the economy. At the same time, the trend has moved towards considerably larger numbers of equations, whether by disaggregation or by inclusion of further economic sectors.

An outstanding example is the Brookings quarterly econometric model of the United States by Duesenberry, Fromm, Klein and Kuh (1965), which was really the result of a cooperative research effort by a large number of research workers. It contains about 150 estimated equations—the exact number depends on choice of alternatives where several are offered—apart from definitional identities and equations with numerical values inserted *a priori*. Economic activity is divided up into 7 industrial sectors: agriculture, durable goods manufacture, non-durables' manufacture, trade, regulated industry, construction, and a residual group. Economic fields covered include consumption, investment in fixed assets and stocks, foreign trade and government transactions; and the equations explaining the volume of activity in various sectors are supplemented by price formation and wage formation equations. The model treats as endogenous some variables usually considered as exogenous such as the size of the labour force and even the number of marriages. Limited-information maximum likelihood is the principal estimation method used.

The classical econometric study in this field based on United Kingdom data is what is usually referred to as the Oxford model, after the Institute in which it was developed by Klein, Ball, Hazlewood and Vandome (1961). Strictly speaking, it consists of two models of which one is based on annual, the other on quarterly data. The annual model, though deserving attention in its own right, was chiefly designed as a pilot study and the relationships were so designed that they permitted adaptation to a quarterly model with variables for which statistical data were available. The quarterly model is more detailed than the annual one, chiefly on account of some disaggregation in the macro-economic totals.

For example, the consumption function in the annual version of the Oxford model expresses real personal consumption as a linear function of real disposable wage income, real disposable non-wage income, and consumption in the previous year. The quarterly model contains four consumption functions referring respectively to food, durables, non-food non-durable goods, and services. In these functions the lagged term is the simple arithmetic average of the consumption term for the last eight quarters; dummy variables are also added for seasonal variation. Otherwise, the equations have the same form as in the annual model.

Some equations presented greater difficulties, for example, the investment function in the annual model could not readily be adapted since no satisfactory quarterly data were available for investment. The quarterly model thus contains no investment function as such; instead, an industrial production equation for capital goods serves the same purpose.

Large-scale economic models continue to be under construction in the United States, the United Kingdom and in other countries. Such models are no longer necessarily considered as final versions once they have been built, as it is now standard practice to modify the equations from time to time on the basis of tests and to re-estimate them with the help of revised and additional data. This means that the construction of large-scale models is an activity absorbing a good deal of time and resources. The United Kingdom study described by Hilton and Heathfield (1970) illustrates modern research in this field and its problems.

7.5 The foreign trade sector

To illustrate the differences in approach which may occur, the way in which imports and exports are treated may be taken as an example. These terms are taken here in the widest sense, embracing not only merchandise trade but also invisible items which enter into the balance of payments.

In (7.7) neither exports nor imports play a part; the absence of these terms constitutes an obvious limitation of Menges' model. Since the balance of payments enters the fundamental national accounts identity connecting national product with consumption, it is clear that a comprehensive model of the economy must include imports and exports, at least implicitly. In (7.5) imports and exports appear as part of the variable G which is formally treated as endogenous, but in fact assumed to follow a law of its own, thus making its contribution to gross national product.

In (7.6) the foreign trade variables form part of the exogenous variable K. The treatment of imports as exogenous implies that the model cannot incorporate an effect upon imports which changes in national product or final demand may have; and this may seriously limit the applicability of the von Hohenbalken–Tintner model. In constructing a model of the United States, the exact nature of the foreign trade relationships is not of crucial importance; but for the economies of the smaller European countries in which foreign trade plays a prominent role the position is different.

It is usual therefore to treat imports as endogenous and to include in the model an import function or several functions. In its simplest form, the relationship gives imports as a linear function of gross national product. This is the treatment of imports in the simple model given by Clark (1949) which in two alternative versions contains 6 or 7 equations, and in the 32-equation model due to Suits (1962).

Exercise 7.4 Consider alternative variables to gross national product and additional variables which may enter into an import function.

In the annual version of the Oxford model, the import function refers to the volume of visible imports only, and the other variables included are the industrial production index, the ratio of the import price index to a price index of final output, and the ratio of gold and dollar reserves at the beginning of the period to the imports in the past two years. This ratio, indicating the state of the balance of payments, is also retained in the three import functions of the quarterly model which refer to food, raw materials, and manufactures, respectively. Otherwise the three import functions contain somewhat different variables, the ratio of import price to general price appearing in the function for manufactures only, and the materials import function containing a stock variable.

The Netherlands Central Planning Bureau model contains only one import function, but it has been most carefully formulated and contains no fewer than seven variables besides the import volume. Instead of one income variable there are two, stockbuilding being treated separately from other final demand, the components of which have been re-weighted according to their import content. In the composite price variable, time-lags have been used for domestic price and indirect taxes in comparison with the import price. There appear two second differences or " quasi-accelerators ", one representing the lead of imports over sales, while the other indicates that inflationary pressure itself exercises an influence on imports. The remaining variables give the effect of quotas and of liberalization of trade.

Whilst the exact form of the import function or functions is open to argument, there seems little doubt about the desirability of treating imports as endogenous. The position is less clear with regard to exports. Whilst production and export prices of the country studied have a bearing on exports, there are other factors in operation which it is less easy to lay a finger on. Such are the volume of demand or foreign trade in the world or in particular countries, export prices of competitor countries, and the promotional sales effort made by the exporting country.

If these external or intangible factors are believed to exercise a more important influence upon exports than the state of the key economic variables at home, then it seems correct to treat exports as exogenous. This procedure has been adopted, for example, in the Klein–Goldberger model for the U.S. and in Narasimham's model for India.

Other models include export functions and treat exports as endogenous. Even so, exogenous variables must enter the export function or functions and play a prominent part therein. In the Brookings model of the U.S., the export function includes real world exports as well as a relative price of U.S. exports and a lagged export term.

7.6 Application to forecasting

The structural equations of a macro-model and the numerical parameter values appearing therein are in themselves of theoretical interest. They give an insight into the way the economy works and may be used in a historical analysis of economic events and their causes. Econometrics and economic history, though often studied by different specialists, may be applied in combination; an example of such a study in the field of imports is one made by Scott (1963).

Another application is in the field of simulation studies designed to uncover the effect of postulated events upon various economic sectors. The model of Duesenberry, Eckstein and Fromm (1960) was especially constructed for this purpose, so as to discover typical patterns in timing and duration of different aspects implied by a recession in the United States.

However, the application upon which the most attention has been focused lies in the field of forecasting, particularly in the short run. It is logical to presume that relationships which have served as a more or less accurate explanation of events in the past will also hold in future. Thus their use in forecasting serves at the same time as a test of their validity.

Before making a forecast, the structural equations are converted into reduced form, if not directly obtained that way, or else they are brought into a form in which the endogenous variables may be deduced step by step from the values of the predetermined variables. Numerical values are then inserted for the latter. This is theoretically a straightforward matter with regard to lagged variables; in practice, owing to delay in publication, even their values may not be available or only in preliminary form. For current exogenous (and as far as required for lagged) variables, estimates are made on the basis of any information that may be available.

As an example, we return once more to Menges' model for Western Germany in numerical form as given in (7.8). By successively eliminating I and Y from the first two equations, and by rearranging the resulting equations and those for C and Q, we obtain the following system for the predicted values:

$$Q_p = -13\cdot98 + \cdot145\ Q_{-1} + \cdot425\ R$$
$$Y_p = -\ 7\cdot63 + \cdot608\ Y_{-1} + 1\cdot594\ Q_p$$
$$I_p = -17\cdot98 - \cdot075\ Y_{-1} + 1\cdot097\ Q_p$$
$$C_p = \quad 32\cdot98 + \cdot157\ C_{-1} - \cdot272\ P + \cdot540\ Y_p$$

The data used for estimation refer to the years 1950–57. To make a forecast for 1958, the 1957 data are used for the lagged terms. With $Q_{-1} = 57\cdot0$, $Y_{-1} = 189\cdot5$, $C_{-1} = 123\cdot0$ the equations become

$$Q_p = -5\cdot72 + \cdot425\ R$$
$$Y_p = 107\cdot59 + 1\cdot594\ Q_p$$
$$I_p = -32\cdot19 + 1\cdot097\ Q_p$$
$$C_p = \quad 52\cdot29 - \cdot272\ P + \cdot540\ Y_p$$

and it only remains to estimate the 1958 values of R and P to obtain the 1958 forecast values for the endogenous variables.

The accuracy of such a forecast depends on the correct specification and estimation of the model, as well as on correct assessment of changes in the exogenous variables. Errors of each kind may creep in, and a forecast made with the aid of an econometric model is not necessarily better than one obtained by other means, using information on all variables from different sources. The main advantage of the econometric approach lies in being systematic and giving logically consistent results, the dependence of which on the assumptions made may be clearly recognized.

Assessments of the performance of the Oxford model, for example, have been made from time to time. The figures given in the table opposite are derived from a study by Vandome (1963), permitting comparison of actual changes in major economic variables with changes predicted by various methods and, incidentally, with a prediction of " no change ". The foreign trade and consumption variables are measured in volume terms.

The relative accuracy of the different predictions varies from series to series, and an overall measure of accuracy would depend on the weight given to each series. On the whole, Vandome concludes that the model compares favourably with the " no change " hypothesis and with straight extrapolation, though an autoregressive equation is a serious rival. None of the methods has a really impressive record.

There has been some discussion not only on the use of econometric models versus other methods for short-term forecasting but also on the suitability of different econometric models. Friend and Jones (1964)

130

Variable	Percentage change between corresponding quarter 1960 and 1961 for the U.K.			
	Estimated with the help of			
	Extra-polation of trend	Auto-regressive equation	Econo-metric model	Actual
1st quarter				
Industrial production	+9·6	+4·7	+1·6	+·6
Unemployment	−26·1	+4·3	+·1	−12·4
Imports	+15·4	+4·1	−2·3	+4·6
Exports	+9·7	+2·6	+1·7	+·5
Food consumption	+3·1	+1·9	+1·4	+2·0
Durables consumption	+16·8	+2·9	−11·4	−11·7
Other consumption	+6·5	+3·9	+·7	+7·5
Output price	+·2	+2·1	−4·3	+1·5
Wage rates	+2·0	+4·0	+5·0	+4·4
Wage earnings	+6·4	+6·6	+3·8	+6·9
2nd quarter				
Industrial production	+9·6	+4·4	+·2	+2·5
Unemployment	−26·3	+15·9	+39·8	−12·7
Imports	+15·3	+3·4	−2·2	−5·0
Exports	+9·7	+3·0	+1·5	+2·7
Food consumption	+3·1	+1·9	−·2	+4·5
Durables consumption	+16·8	+5·1	−8·3	−3·1
Other consumption	+6·5	+3·1	+2·6	−1·6
Output price	+·2	+2·5	+1·7	+5·2
Wage rates	+2·0	+4·5	+5·0	+4·1
Wage earnings	+6·2	+6·6	+2·9	+6·7

argue in favour of small-scale as against large models. To derive predictions for quarterly changes in gross national product and its major
components in the United States, they construct a model consisting of
an identity and four equations for changes in consumption, residential
construction, plant and equipment expenditure, and inventory investment; government expenditure plus net exports is treated as exogenous.
Prominent explanatory variables are number of houses started a quarter

earlier and plant and equipment expenditure anticipated a quarter earlier. The equation for changes in residential construction is simply a linear function of the same variable lagged and lagged changes in houses started.

The implications of such a procedure may be noted. A true structural relationship explaining changes in residential building activity would use such economic variables as an indicator of income, a price term including the rate of interest, and the stock of existing houses. If, however, the explanatory variables used are merely leading indicators, then the equation for building activity is a forecast equation formally treated as a structural relation but not in effect providing an explanation in terms of the economic system.

The econometrician who is concerned with short-term forecasting is thus somewhat in a dilemma. In order to arrive at successful predictions it appears that features of non-econometric forecasting methods have to be incorporated into the model, whilst theoretical considerations may suggest otherwise. It may thus be desirable in model-building to have special regard for the purpose which the model is intended to serve, rather than to attempt the construction of all-purpose models.

It is, of course, not necessary to use prediction equations of a model mechanically. If there is reason to believe that special circumstances operate at a particular time, this information may be incorporated in the forecast equations. In any event, current exogenous variables have to be estimated by non-econometric methods. Thus econometric and other methods may be used in combination rather than as alternatives.

The use of econometric models for medium and long-term forecasting, for which there are fewer practicable alternative methods, is less controversial. Such forecasts are generally conditional forecasts, showing alternative effects of alternative assumptions. Similarly, policy models showing the effect upon the economy of alternative economic policy measures may be constructed by incorporating policy instruments such as taxation rates into the model as exogenous variables.

Such approaches, though promising, are nevertheless fraught with difficulties too. There is no guarantee that structural equations, even if established as holding in the past, will continue to hold in the more distant future. Furthermore, the effect of changes in a policy variable in future can only be accurately assessed if sufficiently wide variations have been experienced in the past to provide a basis for observation. For these and other reasons, econometric models have been used for the purpose of economic policy recommendations, though, with the exception of the Netherlands, not widely for economic policy decisions.

7.7 Conclusion

This brief account of forecasting by means of econometric models and of the problems encountered herein brings to an end the introduction to econometric macro-models and to econometric applications in general. It is not claimed that a detailed or comprehensive account of work done has been given. An attempt has merely been made to show what kind of problems are confronting the applied econometrician and how they may be tackled.

For the student of the subject who wants to go farther, the econometric studies which have been briefly described in the text and which are listed at the end of the book will provide a good deal of reading material which will repay study. In addition, the methodological aspects of the subject are further developed in some of the textbooks and original studies listed.

However, econometrics is a practical subject which cannot be entirely learnt from reading. It has been shown that there are still many tasks ahead. Some of these may call for attack by the specialist academic research worker or even by the research team; but there is also scope for simpler studies which those who are not primarily econometricians may require to carry out.

Modern computers facilitate the carrying out of econometric investigations but do not reduce them to a mechanical routine; econometrics remains an art as well as a science. There can, moreover, be little doubt about the practical importance of the subject. Whatever shortcomings there may be in results obtained hitherto, they only emphasize the need for further effort in a potentially rewarding cause.

ANSWERS TO EXERCISES

7.1

$$b_{RF} = \cdot672$$

or with 95 per cent confidence limits,

$$\cdot571 \leqslant b_{RF} \leqslant \cdot734$$

b_{SE} is upward biased, its point estimate being near the upper 95 per cent confidence limit of b_{RF}. The bias is even more noticeable for the multiplier since

$$1/(1 - b_{SE}) = 3\cdot73$$

7.2

$$b_1 = 1 - 1/2\cdot39 = \cdot582$$
$$b_2 = \cdot37/2\cdot39 = \cdot155$$
$$b_1 + b_2 = \cdot582 + \cdot155 = \cdot737$$

This can be said to represent the long-term propensity to consume, in contrast to the short-term propensity ·58. An increase in income by 100 units raises consumption immediately by 58 units and eventually by 74 units.

7.3 Only the first, second and fourth equations need be considered. There are three predetermined variables in these equations, and an identified equation cannot contain more than four variables. In fact, the equations in question contain only three, so that over-identification may be suspected; and the coefficients matrix of the variables omitted from the first equation Q, Q_{-1}, R is

$$\begin{pmatrix} \beta_3 & 0 & 0 \\ 0 & \gamma_4 & \gamma_5 \end{pmatrix}$$

Two non-vanishing determinants may be constructed; similarly with the coefficients

$$\begin{pmatrix} \gamma_1 & 0 & 0 \\ 0 & \gamma_4 & \gamma_5 \end{pmatrix}$$

7.4 Gross national product might be replaced by national income before or after taxes, or by total final demand; this might be broken down, e.g. into personal consumption, government consumption, investment, and exports. Stock changes could be introduced explicitly, though the causal relation between imports and stocks might be either way.

It seems also natural to take price factors into account, particularly if imports in real terms are studied. A ratio or difference between an import price and a domestic price index seems appropriate. Special factors such as inflationary pressure could also be represented by suitable indicators.

APPENDIX

Lower and upper bound of significance points for Durbin–Watson d-statistic

5 per cent

n	$k = 1$		$k = 2$		$k = 3$	
	d_L	d_U	d_L	d_U	d_L	d_U
15	1·08	1·36	0·95	1·54	0·82	1·75
16	1·10	1·37	0·98	1·54	0·86	1·73
17	1·13	1·38	1·02	1·54	0·90	1·71
18	1·16	1·39	1·05	1·53	0·93	1·69
19	1·18	1·40	1·08	1·53	0·97	1·68
20	1·20	1·41	1·10	1·54	1·00	1·68
21	1·22	1·42	1·13	1·54	1·03	1·67
22	1·24	1·43	1·15	1·54	1·05	1·66
23	1·26	1·44	1·17	1·54	1·08	1·66
24	1·27	1·45	1·19	1·55	1·10	1·66
25	1·29	1·45	1·21	1·55	1·12	1·66
26	1·30	1·46	1·22	1·55	1·14	1·65
27	1·32	1·47	1·24	1·56	1·16	1·65
28	1·33	1·48	1·26	1·56	1·18	1·65
29	1·34	1·48	1·27	1·56	1·20	1·65
30	1·35	1·49	1·28	1·57	1·21	1·65
31	1·36	1·50	1·30	1·57	1·23	1·65
32	1·37	1·50	1·31	1·57	1·24	1·65
33	1·38	1·51	1·32	1·58	1·26	1·65
34	1·39	1·51	1·33	1·58	1·27	1·65
35	1·40	1·52	1·34	1·58	1·28	1·65
36	1·41	1·52	1·35	1·59	1·29	1·65
37	1·42	1·53	1·36	1·59	1·31	1·66
38	1·43	1·54	1·37	1·59	1·32	1·66
39	1·43	1·54	1·38	1·60	1·33	1·66
40	1·44	1·54	1·39	1·60	1·34	1·66
45	1·48	1·57	1·43	1·62	1·38	1·67
50	1·50	1·59	1·46	1·63	1·42	1·67
55	1·53	1·60	1·49	1·64	1·45	1·68
60	1·55	1·62	1·51	1·65	1·48	1·69
65	1·57	1·63	1·54	1·66	1·50	1·70
70	1·58	1·64	1·55	1·67	1·52	1·70
75	1·60	1·65	1·57	1·68	1·54	1·71
80	1·61	1·66	1·59	1·69	1·56	1·72
85	1·62	1·67	1·60	1·70	1·57	1·72
90	1·63	1·68	1·61	1·70	1·59	1·73
95	1·64	1·69	1·62	1·71	1·60	1·73
100	1·65	1·69	1·63	1·72	1·61	1·74

1 per cent

n	k = 1		k = 2		k = 3	
	d_L	d_U	d_L	d_U	d_L	d_U
15	0·81	1·07	0·70	1·25	0·59	1·46
16	0·84	1·09	0·74	1·25	0·63	1·44
17	0·87	1·10	0·77	1·25	0·67	1·43
18	0·90	1·12	0·80	1·26	0·71	1·42
19	0·93	1·13	0·83	1·26	0·74	1·41
20	0·95	1·15	0·86	1·27	0·77	1·41
21	0·97	1·16	0·89	1·27	0·80	1·41
22	1·00	1·17	0·91	1·28	0·83	1·40
23	1·02	1·19	0·94	1·29	0·86	1·40
24	1·04	1·20	0·96	1·30	0·88	1·41
25	1·05	1·21	0·98	1·30	0·90	1·41
26	1·07	1·22	1·00	1·31	0·93	1·41
27	1·09	1·23	1·02	1·32	0·95	1·41
28	1·10	1·24	1·04	1·32	0·97	1·41
29	1·12	1·25	1·05	1·33	0·99	1·42
30	1·13	1·26	1·07	1·34	1·01	1·42
31	1·15	1·27	1·08	1·34	1·02	1·42
32	1·16	1·28	1·10	1·35	1·04	1·43
33	1·17	1·29	1·11	1·36	1·05	1·43
34	1·18	1·30	1·13	1·36	1·07	1·43
35	1·19	1·31	1·14	1·37	1·08	1·44
36	1·21	1·32	1·15	1·38	1·10	1·44
37	1·22	1·32	1·16	1·38	1·11	1·45
38	1·23	1·33	1·18	1·39	1·12	1·45
39	1·24	1·34	1·19	1·39	1·14	1·45
40	1·25	1·34	1·20	1·40	1·15	1·46
45	1·29	1·38	1·24	1·42	1·20	1·48
50	1·32	1·40	1·28	1·45	1·24	1·49
55	1·36	1·43	1·32	1·47	1·28	1·51
60	1·38	1·45	1·35	1·48	1·32	1·52
65	1·41	1·47	1·38	1·50	1·35	1·53
70	1·43	1·49	1·40	1·52	1·37	1·55
75	1·45	1·50	1·42	1·53	1·39	1·56
80	1·47	1·52	1·44	1·54	1·42	1·57
85	1·48	1·53	1·46	1·55	1·43	1·58
90	1·50	1·54	1·47	1·56	1·45	1·59
95	1·51	1·55	1·49	1·57	1·47	1·60
100	1·52	1·56	1·50	1·58	1·48	1·60

REFERENCES

AITCHISON, J. and BROWN, J. A. C. (1957), *The Lognormal Distribution*. Cambridge: University Press.

ALLEN, R. G. D. and BOWLEY, A. L. (1935), *Family Expenditure*. London: P. S. King.

ANDERSON, T. W. and RUBIN, H. (1949), " Estimation of the parameters of a single equation in a complete system of stochastic equations ", *Ann. Math. Stat.*, **20**, 46–63.

ARROW, K. J., CHENERY, H. B., MINHAS, B. and SOLOW, R. M. (1961), " Capital-labour substitution and economic efficiency ", *Rev. Econ. & Stat.*, **43**, 225–250.

AUKRUST, O. (1959), " Investment and economic growth ", *Productivity Measurement Rev.*, No. 16, 35–53.

BARTEN, A. P. (1964), " Consumer demand functions under conditions of almost additive preferences ", *Econometrica*, **32**, 1–38.

BARTLETT, M. S. (1949), " Fitting a straight line if both variables are subject to error ", *Biometrics*, **5**, 207–242.

BASMANN, R. L. (1957), " A generalised classical method of linear estimation of coefficients in a structural equation ", *Econometrica*, **25**, 77–83.

BENTZEL, R. and WOLD, H. (1946), " On statistical demand analysis from the viewpoint of simultaneous equations ", *Skand. Aktuarietidskrift*, **29**, 95–114.

BRIDGE, J. L. (1971), *Applied Econometrics*. Amsterdam: North-Holland Publishing Co.

BRONFENBRENNER, M., and DOUGLAS, P. H. (1939), " Cross section studies in the Cobb–Douglas function ", *Journal of Political Economy*, **47**, 761–785.

BROWN, M. (1966), *On the Theory and Measurement of Technological Change*. Cambridge: University Press.

BROWN, M. and DE CANI, J. S. (1963), " A measure of technological employment ", *Rev. Econ. & Stat.*, **45**, 386–394.

CENTRAL PLANNING BUREAU (1961), *Central Economic Plan, 1961*. The Hague: Government Printing Office.

CENTRAL STATISTICAL OFFICE (1971), *National Income and Expenditure 1971*. London: H.M.S.O.

CENTRAL STATISTICAL OFFICE (1972), *Abstract of Regional Statistics No. 7*. London: H.M.S.O.

CENTRAL STATISTICS OFFICE (1962), *National Income and Expenditure 1961*. Dublin: Stationery Office.

CENTRAL STATISTICS OFFICE (1969), *Household Budget Enquiry 1965–66*. Dublin: Stationery Office.

CHOW, G. C. (1957), *Demand for Automobiles in the United States*. Amsterdam: North Holland Publishing Co.

CHRIST, C. F. (1967), *Econometric Models and Methods*. New York: John Wiley.

CLARK, C. (1949), " A system of equations explaining the United States trade cycle 1921 to 1941 ", *Econometrica*, **17**, 93–124.

COBB, C. W. and DOUGLAS, P. H. (1928), " A theory of production ", *Amer. Economic Rev.*, **18**, suppl., 139–165.

CRAGG, J. G. (1967), " On the relative small-sample properties of several structural-equation estimators ", *Econometrica*, **35**, 89–110.

CRAMER, J. S. (1962), *The Ownership of Major Consumer Durables*. Cambridge: University Press.

CRAMER, J. S. (1969), *Empirical Econometrics*. Amsterdam: North-Holland Publishing Co.

DAVIS, H. T. (1941), *Theory of Econometrics*. Bloomington, Indiana: Principia Press.

DEAN, J. (1936), *Statistical Determination of Costs with Special Reference to Marginal Cost*. Chicago: University Press.

DEAN, J. (1942), " Department store cost functions ", *Studies in Mathematical Economics and Econometrics in Memory of Henry Schultz* (ed. Lange, McIntyre and Jutema, Chicago: University Press), 222–254.

DERKSEN, J. B. D. (1940), " Long cycles in residential building: an explanation ", *Econometrica*, **8**, 97–116.

137

DOUGLAS, P. H. (1934), *The Theory of Wages.* New York: Macmillan.
DOUGLAS, P. H. (1948), " Are there laws of production? ", *Amer. Economic Rev.,* **38,** 1–41.
DUESENBERRY, J. S. (1949), *Income, Saving and the Theory of Consumer Behaviour.* Cambridge, Mass.: Harvard University Press.
DUESENBERRY, J. S., ECKSTEIN, O. and FROMM, G. (1960), " A simulation of the United States economy in recession ", *Econometrica,* **28,** 749–809.
DUESENBERRY, J. S., FROMM, G. C., KLEIN, L. R., KUH, E. and contributors (1965), *The Brookings Quarterly Econometric Model of the United States.* Amsterdam: North-Holland Publishing Co.
DURBIN, J. and WATSON, G. S. (1950, 1951), " Testing for serial correlation in least-squares regression ", *Biometrika,* **37,** 409–428; **38,** 159–178.
ENGEL, E. (1895), " Die Produktions- und Consumptionsverhältnisse des Königreichs Sachsen ", *Bulletin de l'Institut international de Statistique,* **9,** Appendix, pp. 1–54 (reprinted).
EZEKIEL, M. and FOX, K. A. (1959), *Methods of Correlation and Regression Analysis,* 3rd edn. New York/London: John Wiley/Chapman & Hall.
FORSYTH, F. G. (1960), " The relationship between family size and family expenditure ", *J. Roy. Stat. Soc.,* Series A. **123,** 367–397.
FRIEDMAN, M. (1957), *A Theory of the Consumption Function.* Princeton: University Press.
FRIEND, I. and JONES, R. C. (1964), " Short-run forecasting models incorporating anticipatory data ", *Models of Income Determination* (National Bureau of Economic Research, Princeton University Press), 279–326.
FRISCH, R. (1933), *Pitfalls in the Statistical Construction of Demand and Supply Curves.* Leipzig: Hans Buske.
FRISCH, R. (1934), *Statistical Confluence Analysis by means of Complete Regression Systems.* Oslo: Universitets Økonomiske Institutt.
FRISCH, R. (1959), " A complete scheme for computing all direct and cross demand elasticities in a model with many sectors ", *Econometrica,* **27,** 177–196.
GALLAWAY, L. E. and SMITH, P. E. (1961), " A quarterly econometric model of the United States ", *J. Amer. Stat. Assoc.,* **56,** 379–383.
GEARY, R. C. (1949), " Determination of linear relations between systematic parts of variables with errors of observations, the variances of which are unknown ", *Econometrica,* **17,** 30–58.
GEARY, R. C. (1963), " Some results about relations between stochastic variables: a discussion document ", *Rev. Intern. Stat. Inst.,* **31,** 163–181.
GIRSHICK, M. A. and HAAVELMO, T. (1947), " Statistical analysis of the demand for food: examples of simultaneous estimation of structural equations ", *Econometrica,* **15,** 79–110.
GOLDBERGER, A. S. (1964), *Econometric Theory.* New York, London, Sydney: John Wiley.
GOLLNICK, H. (1959), *Ausgaben und Verbrauch in Abhängigkeit von Einkommen und Haushaltsstruktur.* Hannover: Alfred Strothe (Agrarwirtschaft, Sonderheft 6/7).
GRILICHES, Z. (1963), " The sources of measured productivity growth: United States agriculture, 1940–1960 ", *J. Pol. Econ.,* **71,** 331–346.
GRILICHES, Z. and RINGSTAD, V. (1971), *Economies of Scale and the Form of the Production Function.* Amsterdam: North-Holland Publishing Co.
HAAVELMO, T. (1943), " The statistical implications of a system of simultaneous equations ", *Econometrica,* **11,** 1–12.
HAAVELMO, T. (1947), " Methods of measuring the marginal propensity to consume ", *J. Amer. Stat. Assoc.,* **42,** 105–122.
HEADY, E. O. (1946), " Production functions from a random sample of farms ", *J. Farm Economics,* **28,** 989–1004.
HEADY, E. O. and DILLON, J. L. (1961), *Agricultural Production Functions.* Ames: Iowa State University Press.
HEADY, E. O. and PESEK, J. (1960), " Expansion paths for some production functions ", *Econometrica,* **28,** 900–908.
HILTON, K., and HEATHFIELD, D. F. and contributors (1970), *The Econometric Study of the United Kingdom.* London: Macmillan.

HOHENBALKEN, B. VON and TINTNER, G. (1962), " Econometric models of the
O.E.E.C. member countries, the United States and Canada and their application
to economic policy ", *Weltwirtschaftliches Archiv*, **89**, 29–86.
HOUTHAKKER, H. S. (1957), " An international comparison of household expenditure
patterns, commemorating the centenary of Engel's law ", *Econometrica*, **25**,
532–551.
HOUTHAKKER, H. S. and TAYLOR, L. D. (1966), " Consumer demand in the United
States 1929–1970 ". Cambridge, Mass.: Harvard University Press.
JOHANSEN, L. (1961), " A method for separating the effects of capital accumulation
and shifts in production functions upon growth in labour productivity ",
Economic J., **71**, 775–782.
JOHNSTON, J. (1960), *Statistical Cost Functions*. New York: McGraw-Hill.
JOHNSTON, J. (1972), *Econometric Methods*, 2nd ed. New York: McGraw-Hill.
KENDALL, M. G. (1961), *A Course in Multivariate Analysis*. London: Griffin.
KLEIN, L. R. (1950), *Economic Fluctuations in the United States, 1921–1941*. New
York/London: John Wiley/Chapman & Hall.
KLEIN, L. R. (1962), *An Introduction to Econometrics*. London: Prentice-Hall.
KLEIN, L. R., BALL, R. J., HAZLEWOOD, A. and VANDOME, P. (1961), *An Econometric
Model of the United Kingdom*. Oxford: Basil Blackwell.
KLEIN, L. R. and GOLDBERGER, A. S. (1955). *An Econometric Model of the United
States, 1929–52*. Amsterdam: North-Holland Publishing Co.
KMENTA, J. (1967), " On the estimation of the CES production function ", *Internat.
Econ. Rev.*, **8**, 180–189.
KOOPMANS, T. C. (1949), " Identification problems in economic model construction ",
Econometrica, **17**, 125–144.
KOOPMANS, T. C. and HOOD, W. C. (1953), " The estimation of simultaneous linear
economic relationships ", *Studies in Econometric Method* (ed. Hood and
Koopmans, New York/London: John Wiley/Chapman & Hall), 112–199.
KOYCK, L. M. (1954), *Distributed Lags and Investment Analysis*. Amsterdam:
North-Holland Publishing Co.
LEONTIEF, W. W. (1951), *Structure of the American Economy, 1919–29*, 2nd edn.
New York: Oxford University Press.
LESER, C. E. V. (1954), " Production functions for the British industrial economy ",
Applied Stat., **3**, 174–183.
LESER, C. E. V. (1960), " Demand functions for nine commodity groups in
Australia ", *Australian J. of Stat.*, **2**, 102–113.
LESER, C. E. V. (1971a), " Econometric theory and method ", *The Use of Economics
Literature* (ed. Fletcher, London: Butterworths), 214–223.
LESER, C. E. V. (1971b), " Stocks of durable goods in a complete demand system ",
Bulletin of Economic Research, **23**, 129–140.
LINDLEY, D. V., and MILLER, J. C. P. (1953), *Cambridge Elementary Statistical
Tables*. Cambridge: University Press.
LIU, T. C. (1960), " Underidentification, structural estimation and forecasting ",
Econometrica, **28**, 855–865.
LIVIATAN, N. (1961), " Errors in variables and Engel curves analysis ", *Econometrica*,
29, 336–362.
LOMAX, K. S. (1949), " An agricultural production function for the U.K., 1924–
1947 ", *Manchester School*, **17**, 146–162.
LOMAX, K. S. (1950), " Coal production functions for Great Britain ", *J. Roy. Stat.
Soc.*, Series A, **113**, 346–351.
MALINVAUD, E. (1970), *Statistical Methods of Econometrics*, 2nd ed. Amsterdam:
North-Holland Publishing Co.
MARSCHAK, J., and ANDREWS, W. H. (1944), " Random simultaneous equations and
the theory of production ", *Econometrica*, **12**, 143–205.
MENDERSHAUSEN, H. (1938), " On the significance of Professor Douglas' production
function ", *Econometrica*, **6**, 143–153.
MENGES, G. (1959), " Ein ökonometrisches Modell der Bundesrepublik Deutschland
(Vier Strukturgleichungen) ", *I.F.O.-Studien*, **5**, 1–22.
MINCER, J. (1963), " Market prices, opportunity costs and income effects ",
Measurement in Economics (Stanford: University Press), 67–82.

MODIGLIANI, F. (1949), "Fluctuations in the saving-income ratio: a problem in economic forecasting", *Studies in Income and Wealth*, 11 (New York: National Bureau of Economic Research), 371–443.

MOORE, H. L. (1914), *Economic Cycles: their Law and Cause*. New York: Macmillan.

MOORE, H. L. (1917), *Forecasting the Yield and Price of Cotton*. New York: Macmillan.

MORONEY, J. R. (1970), "Identification and specification analysis of alternative equations for estimating the elasticity of substitution", *Southern Econ. J.*, 36, 287–299.

MURDOCH, J., and BARNES, J. A. (1968), *Statistical Tables for Science and Engineering*. London: Macmillan.

MURTI, V. N. and SASTRY, V. K. (1957), "Production functions for Indian industry", *Econometrica*, 25, 205–221.

MUTH, R. F. (1960), "The demand for non-farm housing", *The Demand for Durable Goods* (ed. Harberger, Chicago: University Press), 27–96.

NARASIMHAM, N. V. A. (1956), *A Short-term Planning Model for India*. Amsterdam: North-Holland Publishing Co.

NERLOVE, M. (1958), *Distributed Lags and Demand Analysis for Agricultural and other Commodities*. Washington: U.S. Department of Agriculture.

NERLOVE, M. (1967), "Recent empirical studies of the CES and related production functions", *The Theory and Empirical Analysis of Production* (ed. BROWN, New York: National Bureau of Economic Research), 55–136.

OLSON, E. C. (1948), "Factors affecting international differences in production", *Amer. Econ. Rev.*, 38, suppl., 502–522.

ORGANISATION FOR ECONOMIC COOPERATION AND DEVELOPMENT (1966), *Economic Growth 1960–1970*. Paris: OECD.

PEARCE, I. F. (1964), *A Contribution to Demand Analysis*. Oxford: Clarendon Press.

PHELPS BROWN, E. H. and HANDFIELD-JONES, S. J. (1952), "The climacteric of the 1890s: a study in the expanding economy", *Oxford Economic Papers*, new series, 4, 266–307.

POWELL, A. (1966), "A complete system of consumer demand equations for the Australian economy fitted by a model of additive preferences", *Econometrica*, 34, 661–675.

PRAIS, S. J., and HOUTHAKKER, H. S. (1971), *The Analysis of Family Budgets*, 2nd ed. Cambridge: University Press.

REIERSØL, O. (1945), *Confluence Analysis by means of Instrumental Sets of Variables*. Stockholm: Almqvist & Wiksell.

ROOS, C. F. and SZELISKI, V. VON (1939), "Factors governing changes in domestic automobile demand", *The Dynamics of Automobile Demand* (New York: General Motors, 21–95.)

SCHULTZ, H. (1938), *The Theory and Measurement of Demand*. Chicago: University Press.

SCOTT, M. FG. (1963), *A Study of United Kingdom Imports*. Cambridge: University Press.

SOLOW, R. M. (1957), "Technical change and the aggregate production function", *Rev. Econ. & Stat.*, 39, 312–320.

STOJKOWICZ, G. (1964), "Market models for agricultural products", *Econometric Model Building* (ed. Wold, Amsterdam: North-Holland Publishing Co.), 386–419.

STONE, J. R. N. (1945), "The analysis of market demand", *J. Roy. Stat. Soc.*, Series A, 108, 286–391.

STONE, J. R. N. (1954a), "The Measurement of Consumers' Expenditure and Behaviour in the United Kingdom", 1920–1938 1, Cambridge: University Press.

STONE, J. R. N. (1954b), "Linear expenditure systems and demand analysis: an application to the pattern of British demand", *Econ. J.*, 64, 511–527.

STONE, J. R. N. and ROWE, D. A. (1958), "Dynamic demand functions: some econometric results", *Economic J.*, 68, 256–270.

STONE, J. R. N. and ROWE, D. A. (1960), "The durability of consumers' durable goods", *Econometrica*, 28, 407–416.

STONE, J. R. N.and STONE, M. W. (1938), " The marginal propensity to consume and the multiplier: a statistical investigation ", *Rev. Economic Studies*, **6**, 1–24.

SUITS, D. B. (1962), " Forecasting and analysis with an econometric model ", *Amer. Economic Rev.*, **52**, 104–132.

SUMMERS, R. (1965), " A capital-intensive approach to the small sample properties of various simultaneous equation estimators ", *Econometrica*, **33**, 1–41.

THEIL, H. (1961), *Economic Forecasts and Policy*, 2nd ed. Amsterdam: North-Holland Publishing Co.

THEIL, H. and NAGAR, A. L. (1961), " Testing the independence of regression disturbances ", *J. Amer. Stat. Assoc.*, **56**, 793–806.

TINBERGEN, J. (1939), *Business Cycles in the United States of America, 1919–32.* Geneva: League of Nations.

TINTNER, G. (1940), *The Variate Difference Method.* Bloomington, Indiana: Principia Press.

TINTNER, G. (1944), " A note on the derivation of production functions from farm records ", *Econometrica*, **12**, 26–34.

TINTNER, G. (1951), " Static econometric models and their empirical verification, illustrated by a study of the American meat market ", *Metroeconomica*, **2**, 172–181.

TINTNER, G. and BROWNLEE, O. L. H. (1944), " Production functions derived from farm records ", *J. Farm Economics*, **26**, 566–571.

VANDOME, P. (1963), " Econometric Forecasting for the United Kingdom ", *Bull. Oxford Univ. Inst. of Econ. & Stat.*, **25**, 239–281.

WALD, A. (1940), " The fitting of straight lines if both variables are subject to error ", *Ann. Math. Stat.*, **11**, 284–300.

WALL, B. (1948), " A Cobb–Douglas function for the United States manufacturing and mining sector 1920–1940 ", *Econometrica*, **16**, 211–213.

WALTERS, A. A. (1963), " Production and cost functions: an econometric survey ", *Econometrica*, **31**, 1–66.

WALTERS, A. A. (1970), *An Introduction to Econometrics*, 2nd ed. London: Macmillan.

WILLIAMS, E. J. (1959), *Regression Analysis*. New York/London: John Wiley. Chapman & Hall.

WILSON, T. A. and ECKSTEIN, O. (1964), " Short-run productivity behavior in U.S. manufacturing ", *Rev. Econ. & Stat.*, **46**, 41–56.

WOLD, H. (1959), " A case-study of interdependent versus causal chain systems ", *Rev. Internat. Stat. Inst.*, **26**, 5–25.

WOLD, H. and JURÉEN, L. (1953), *Demand Analysis—a Study in Econometrics*. New York/Stockholm: John Wiley/Almqvist & Wiksell.

WORKING, E. (1927), " What do statistical demand curves show? ", *Q. J. of Economics*, **41**, 215–235.

WORKING, H. (1943), " Statistical laws of family expenditure ", *J. Amer. Stat. Assoc.*, **38**, 43–56.

YULE, G. U. (1926), " Why do we sometimes get nonsense correlations between time series? A study in sampling and the nature of time series ", *J. Roy. Stat. Soc.*, **89**, 1–69.

ZELLNER, A. (1957), " The short-run consumption function ", *Econometrica*, **25**, 552–567.

ZELLNER, A., HUANG, D. S., and CHAU, L. C. (1965), " Further analysis of the short-run consumption function with emphasis on the role of liquid assets ", *Econometrica*, **33**, 571–581.

ZELLNER, A. and THEIL, H. (1962), " Three-stage least squares: simultaneous estimation of simultaneous relations ", *Econometrica*, **30**, 54–78.

INDEX

144